# Impact of ICT on Library System

# Impact of ICT on Library System

*Edited by*

**Dr Kalpana Gayakwad**
*Chief Librarian*
Dev Sanskriti Vishwavidyalaya

ALLIED PUBLISHERS PVT. LTD.

Noida • Mumbai • Kolkata • Chennai • Bangalore

**ALLIED PUBLISHERS PRIVATE LIMITED**

D-5, Sector-2, **Noida**–201 301
Ph. Nos.: 0120-4320295/2542557/4352866 • E-mail: delhi.books@alliedpublishers.com

17 Chittaranjan Avenue, **Kolkata**–700072
Ph.: 033-22129618 • E-mail: cal.books@alliedpublishers.com

15 J.N. Heredia Marg, Ballard Estate, **Mumbai**–400001
Ph.: 022-42126969 • E-mail: mumbai.books@alliedpublishers.com

No. 25/10, Commander-in-Chief Road, Ethiraj Lane (Next to Post Office)
Egmore, **Chennai**–600008
Ph.: 044-28223938 • E-mail: chennai.books@alliedpublishers.com

P.B. No. 9932, No. 15, 3rd Floor (Next to Vijaya Bank), 5th Cross, Gandhinagar,
Karnataka, **Bangalore**–560009, Ph.: 080-41530285 / 22386239
E-mail: bngl.journals@alliedpublishers.com / apsabng@airtelmail.in

**Website: www.alliedpublishers.com**



ISBN: 978-93-90951-63-5

# प्रस्तावना

कुलपिता पं. श्रीराम शर्मा आचार्य जी का स्वप्न था कि भारत में ऐसा विश्वविद्यालय होना चाहिए जो नालंदा तक्षशिला स्तर का हो, जहाँ से विद्यार्जन कर विद्यार्थी सम्पूर्ण विश्व में ज्ञान की अलख जगाएँ। भारतीय तत्वदर्शन वेद, शास्त्र, पुराण, उपनिषद आदि आध्यात्मिक ज्ञान को जन–जन में पहुँचा कर लोगों को जागृत करें। मानव आज की भौतिकता की चका–चौंध में जीवन मूल्य क्या है? उसे भूल गया है। इसे पुनः प्रतिस्थापित करने के लिए गुरूवर ने देव संस्कृति विश्वविद्यालय की स्थापना की ।

पुज्य गुरूवर के सूक्ष्म सरंक्षण एवं विश्वविद्यालय कुलाधिपति श्रद्धेय डॉ0 प्रणव पण्ड्या जी, गायत्री परिवार की संरक्षिका श्रद्धेया शैल बाला पण्ड्या जी के आशीर्वाद, कुलपति जी का मार्गदर्शन एवं प्रतिकुलपति डॉ.चिन्मय पण्ड्या जी जिनका पग–पग पर दिशा निर्देशन और सहयोग प्राप्त कर हमने संगोष्ठी को सफलता पूर्वक आयोजित किया। वर्तमान युग "साहित्य विस्फोट का युग" है पुस्तकालयों में हजारों लाखों सूचनाओं के भण्डार है ऐसे में साहित्य विस्फोट के युग मे पुस्तकालयध्यक्ष एवं पुस्तकालय कर्मियों के सामने सूचना सम्प्रेषण, सूचना अधिगम, संसाधनों के प्रबंधन, हाउस कीपिग संचालन, पुस्तकालय में संसाधनों की सुरक्षा कार्य प्रणाली एवं डॉ0 एस.आर रंगनाथन के पांच सूत्रों को पूरा करने में सूचना सम्प्रेषण तकनीक ने महत्वपूर्ण भूमिका निभायी है। इन जटिल विषयों पर देव संस्कृति विश्वविद्यालय के केन्द्रीय पुस्तकालय ने राष्ट्रीय संगोष्ठी के माध्यम से पुस्तकालय विज्ञान के विशेषज्ञों ने प्रतिभागियों के समक्ष अपने–अपने विचार एवं अनुभवों को साझा किया, इस संगोष्ठी में मुख्य थीम को दस सब थीम में विभक्त किया। भारत के विभिन्न राज्यों से उन्तीस शोध पत्र प्रप्त हुए जिनमें से 15 शोध पत्रों का चयन किया।

# आभार

संगोष्ठी के सम्पन्न होने में, देव संस्कृति विश्वविद्यालय के उन सभी विद्वत जनों का, पुस्तकालय के सभी सहयोगियों का, कम्प्यूटर सांइस एवं पत्रकारिता के उन सभी छात्र–छात्राओं का जिन्होंने अपना अथक सहयोग प्रदान कर अपना अमूल्य समय दिया।

विशेष रूप से राजा राम मोहन रॉय लाईब्रेरी ऑफ फाउण्डेशन मिनिस्ट्री ऑफ कल्चर के डॉ. ए.पी. सिंह एवं इसरो और इनफ्लिबनेट के भूतपूर्व प्रशासनिक अधिकारी डॉ0 डी. पी. नेगी का बहुत–बहुत आभार प्रकट करती हूँ। साथ ही इनफॉर्मेशन ऑफ लाईब्रेरी नेटवर्क सेंटर– यू जी सी के साइंटिस्ट डॉ. एच.जी होसामणी, हरियाणा केन्द्रीय विश्वविद्यालय के उप पुस्तकालयाध्यक्ष डॉ. राजीव वशिष्ठ एवं गुरूकुल कांगडी विश्वविद्यालय के डॉ0 अनिल धीमान का भी आभार व्यक्त करती हूँ । आप सभी की महती भूमिका एवं सहयोग से यह कार्यक्रम अपनी अभूत पूर्व सफलता के साथ सम्पन्न हुआ आप सभी को मैं पुनः बहुत–बहुत धन्यवाद देती हूँ।

# Contents

## Abstracts

# Contributed Papers

# Transforming Library Systems with the help of Generative Pre-trained Transformer Model

**Sharad Raj Singh Maurya***

**Abstract**

The impact of advanced natural language processing (NLP) techniques, specifically Generative Pre-trained Transformer (GPT), on library systems has been investigated in this study. This research examines how GPT can transform library systems and improve information retrieval and user services. In recent years, the use of Information and Communication Technologies (ICT) has revolutionized library systems. With natural language processing (NLP) being one of the most notable development, Deep learning models such as GPT (Generative Pre-trained Transformer) can enable libraries to efficiently manage and analyse large volumes of text-based information, leading to improved accessibility and usability of library resources. The incorporation of GPT in library systems can lead to improved efficiency and accuracy in cataloguing and classification. By using this transformer model to analyse and categorize books and other materials based on their content, libraries can create more accurate and reliable catalogues, making it easier for users to find the resources they need. Moreover, it can be applied in the creation of digital archives by analysing and categorizing large volumes of text-based data as a result libraries can create comprehensive and easily searchable digital archives that are useful to researchers and scholars who require access to a wide range of historical and cultural materials. This research also goes through some of the tests that were performed to show how GPT can be used to generate metadata and the summarization of various texts.

***Keywords:*** *GPT Models, Natural Language Processing, Information and Communication Technologies.*

---

* MCA (Data Science), Dev Sanskriti Vishwavidyalaya, Haridwar, India.
E-mail: iamsharadraj@gmail.com

## INTRODUCTION

In this study, the impact of advanced natural language processing (NLP) techniques, particularly Generative Pre-trained Transformer (GPT), on library systems has been investigated. The research examines how GPT can transform library systems and improve information retrieval and user services, with a specific focus on cataloguing, generating metadata, references, links to similar sources, and other key areas where GPT excels.

To evaluate the performance of GPT in library systems, a test was conducted using large datasets. The results showed that GPT was able to efficiently manage and analyse large volumes of text-based information, leading to improved accessibility and usability of library resources. By using GPT to analyse and categorize books and other materials based on their content, libraries can create more accurate and reliable catalogues, making it easier for users to find the resources they need.

Moreover, GPT's ability to generate metadata and references can help libraries provide users with a comprehensive understanding of the resources available. The model's capacity to analyse and categorize text-based data can also be used in the creation of digital archives, making it easier for researchers and scholars to access a wide range of historical and cultural materials.

Overall, this study highlights the significant potential of GPT in transforming library systems and improving the user experience. By using advanced transformer models such as GPT, libraries can efficiently manage and analyse large volumes of text-based information, leading to improved accessibility and usability of library resources.

## OVERVIEW OF LIBRARY SYSTEMS AND THEIR CHALLENGES

Libraries have long been regarded as revered institutions, serving as gatekeepers of knowledge and culture. However, with the advent of the digital revolution, traditional library systems face inherent challenges in adapting to the modern era. One of the key challenges lies in the limitations of their search capabilities. Users often struggle to navigate the vast collections and find the specific information they seek efficiently. Moreover, the lack of personalized services in traditional library systems hinders the user experience, as individuals have different preferences, interests, and needs.

Additionally, the explosion of information available online poses significant hurdles for libraries in curating and providing access to relevant resources. The sheer volume and diversity of online information make it challenging for libraries to ensure the accuracy, quality, and comprehensiveness of their collections. As a result, users may feel overwhelmed and struggle to discern trustworthy and valuable sources from the vast sea of information available.

## INTRODUCTION TO GENERATIVE PRE-TRAINED TRANSFORMER MODELS

GPT models have emerged as a remarkable breakthrough in the field of natural language processing, revolutionizing the way computers comprehend and generate human-like text. These models have garnered immense attention and acclaim due to their ability to generate coherent and contextually appropriate text, making them invaluable in numerous applications.

At the core of GPT models lies a self-attention mechanism inspired by the Transformer architecture, enabling them to effectively capture intricate patterns and contextual relationships between words. This advanced technology leverages extensive pre-training on massive amounts of text data, allowing GPT models to learn from a diverse range of sources and languages. The vast training corpus ensures that GPT models grasp the subtleties of human language, enabling them to produce more human-like text.

GPT models have been trained on a wide array of publicly available text sources, such as books, websites, and articles, providing them with a wealth of linguistic knowledge. For example, OpenAI's GPT-3, one of the most prominent GPT models, was trained on a corpus of over 570GB of text data (Brown *et al.*, 2020). This vast dataset encompasses various genres and domains, enabling GPT models to have a broad understanding of different topics and writing styles.

The effectiveness of GPT models in understanding and generating text can be attributed to their ability to capture dependencies between words through the self-attention mechanism. By attending to different parts of the input text, GPT models can model long-range dependencies and contextual information effectively. This mechanism allows GPT models to generate text that flows coherently and exhibits contextually appropriate responses.

GPT models have showcased impressive performance in a range of natural language processing tasks. For instance, they have been successful in machine translation, achieving competitive results on benchmark datasets such as the WMT 2014 English-to-German translation task (Vaswani *et al.*, 2017). GPT models have also demonstrated their proficiency in sentiment analysis, accurately identifying the sentiment expressed in textual content (Radford *et al.*, 2017). Furthermore, GPT models have shown their creative capabilities by generating imaginative pieces of writing, including poetry and storylines (Gao *et al.*, 2020).

The transformative potential of GPT models is evident across various industries and domains. In libraries, GPT models can aid in automating tasks such as cataloguing, recommending books based on user preferences, and generating summaries for academic papers or literary works. Their ability to understand and generate human-like text makes them valuable tools for natural language understanding and generation in information-intensive environments.

It's worth noting that while GPT models have achieved remarkable results, they are not without limitations. They may occasionally generate text that is grammatically correct but semantically incorrect or lacks factual accuracy. Researchers and developers continue to explore techniques to mitigate these issues and improve the robustness and reliability of GPT models.

## CONCEPTUAL FRAMEWORK FOR TRANSFORMING LIBRARY SYSTEMS WITH GPT MODEL

(a) **Define Objectives:** First step in the framework world be defining out objective. For example, the objectives may include improving personalized recommendations, enhancing user interactions through virtual assistants, or automating certain library processes.

(b) **Data Collection:** Gather relevant data from library catalogues, user interactions, and books, research papers, user's past issues in a library, etc. This data will be used for training the GPT model. Ensure that the data is comprehensive, diverse, and representative of the library's content and user preferences.

(c) **Pre-process Data:** Clean and pre-process the collected data. This involves tasks such as removing duplicates, formatting the data, and tokenizing text into appropriate units (e.g., words or sub words) for input into the GPT model. Pre-processing may also involve data augmentation techniques to increase the training data's diversity, one possibility is the usage of vector databases for better results.

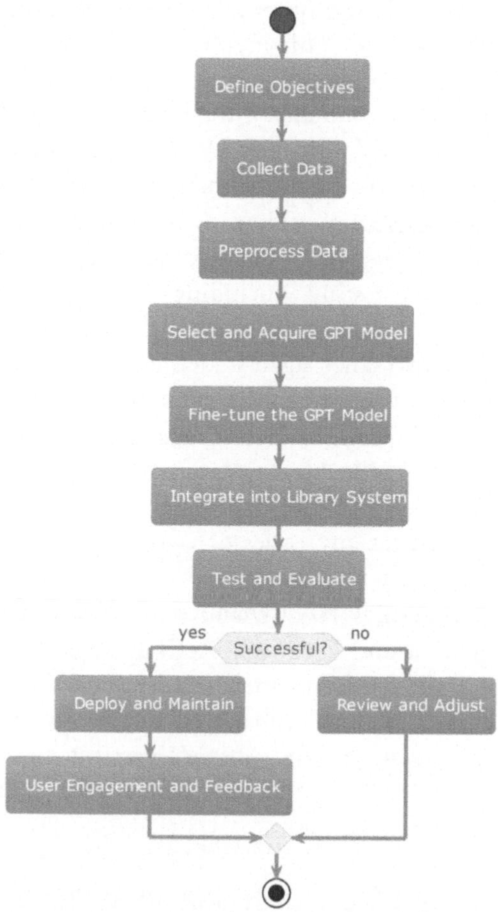


**Figure 1:** Conceptual Framework

(d) **Select and Acquire GPT Model:** Choose an appropriate GPT model based on the library's requirements, available resources, and the specific task at hand. GPT models such as GPT-2 or GPT-3 are commonly used, but newer model like GPT-4 may also be considered.

(e) **Fine-tune the GPT Model:** Fine-tuning is the process of adapting the pre-trained GPT model to the library's specific context and data. This involves training the GPT model on the library's data to capture domain-specific patterns and improve performance for the intended tasks. Fine-tuning may require specialized hardware and significant computational resources.

(f) **Integration into Library System:** Integrate the trained GPT model into the library system. This involves developing appropriate APIs or service layers that enable communication between the GPT model and other components of the library system. The integration should be designed to seamlessly incorporate GPT-based functionalities into the existing library interfaces or platforms.

(g) **Testing and Evaluation:** Thoroughly test the integrated GPT model to ensure its functionality, accuracy, and performance. Conduct rigorous testing, including both automated tests and human evaluations, to validate the GPT model's outputs. Evaluate the model's performance against defined metrics and gather user feedback to assess its effectiveness and user satisfaction.

(h) **Deployment and Maintenance:** Once the GPT model has been tested and validated, deploy it within the library system. Continuously monitor and maintain the model to ensure its performance, address any issues or errors, and incorporate updates as needed. Regularly retrain or fine-tune the model using new data to adapt to changing library dynamics and user preferences.

(i) **User Engagement and Feedback:** Actively engage with library users to gather feedback on their experiences with GPT-based functionalities. Use this feedback to further improve the system, refine recommendations, and enhance user interactions. Encourage users to provide feedback and iterate on the implementation based on their needs and suggestions.

## APPLICATIONS OF GPT MODELS IN LIBRARY SYSTEMS

### (a) Personalized Recommendations

By analysing user preferences, browsing history, and feedback, GPT models can generate highly tailored and contextually relevant recommendations. Leveraging the vast amount of data available in library catalogues and user interactions, GPT models can suggest books, articles, or other resources that align with the individual user's interests. The data collected from user interactions, such as borrowing history, search queries, and ratings, is used to train the GPT model and create personalized recommendation algorithms. Additionally, vector databases can be employed to represent library resources and user preferences as vectors, enabling efficient similarity matching and generating accurate recommendations based on content similarities or user behaviour patterns.

### (b) Virtual Assistants

Integrating GPT models into library systems enables the development of virtual assistants that can provide instant and accurate responses to user queries. GPT models excel in understanding natural language, allowing virtual assistants to engage in more conversational and interactive interactions with library patrons. Users can interact with the virtual assistant by asking questions, seeking guidance on research topics, or requesting information about library services. The virtual assistant utilizes the trained GPT model to comprehend and generate appropriate responses. Data from user queries, user feedback, and past interactions can be utilized to improve the performance of the virtual assistant over time, enabling it to provide more accurate and contextually relevant responses.

### (c) Summarization

GPT models can contribute to automatic summarization of text in library systems. With the increasing amount of textual information available, summarization becomes crucial for efficient information retrieval and consumption. GPT models can analyse and comprehend lengthy texts, extracting key information and generating concise summaries. By utilizing GPT models for text summarization, library systems can provide users with condensed versions of articles, research papers, or other text-based resources, enabling them to quickly grasp the main ideas and determine relevance before diving into detailed reading.

### (d) Describing Figures & Images

GPT models can be used to describe figures and images in library systems. Visual materials, such as diagrams, maps, and historical photographs, play a crucial role in various disciplines. By integrating GPT models with image recognition and understanding algorithms, library systems can generate accurate and informative descriptions of visual content. GPT models analyse the visual features and contextual information associated with the figures and images to generate textual descriptions. This functionality enhances accessibility for visually impaired users and provides valuable information to all users about the visual materials available in the library.

User Below is part of the InstuctGPT paper. Could you read and summarize it to me?

GPT-4 The InstructGPT paper focuses on training large language models to follow instructions with human feedback. The authors note that making language models larger doesn't inherently make them better at following a user's intent. Large models can generate outputs that are untruthful, toxic, or simply unhelpful.

To address this issue, the authors fine-tune language models on a wide range of tasks using human feedback. They start with a set of labeler-written prompts and responses, then collect a dataset of labeler demonstrations of the desired model behavior. They fine-tune GPT-3 using supervised learning and then use reinforcement learning from human feedback to further fine-tune the model. The resulting model, called InstructGPT, shows improvements in truthfulness and reductions in toxic output generation while having minimal performance regressions on public NLP datasets.

The authors conclude that fine-tuning with human feedback is a promising direction for aligning language models with human intent.

User Could you explain the process described in Figure 2?

GPT-4 Figure 2 in the InstructGPT paper illustrates the three steps of their method:

1. Supervised fine-tuning (SFT): They collect demonstration data, which consists of labeler-written prompts and desired output behavior. This data is used to fine-tune GPT-3 with supervised learning.

2. Reward model (RM) training: They collect comparison data, where a labeler ranks the outputs from several model samples (from best to worst). This data is used to train the reward model.

3. Reinforcement learning using Proximal Policy Optimization (PPO): They optimize a policy against the reward model using reinforcement learning. For each new prompt sampled from the dataset, the policy generates an output. The reward model calculates a reward for the output, and the reward is used to update the policy using the PPO algorithm.

These three steps are iteratively performed to train the InstructGPT model, which aims to generate outputs that align better with human preferences and follow instructions more effectively.

**Figure 1**

*The above figure from the GPT-4 Technical Report published by Open AI shows how well the GPT-4 model can understand and describe a complex diagram that would be otherwise difficult to understand for newcomers.*

## (e) Translation of Language

Libraries often encounter diverse language materials, including books, articles, and manuscripts. GPT models, trained on multilingual corpora, can effectively translate text from one language to another. By employing GPT models for translation tasks, library systems can facilitate access to a wider range of resources for users who may not be proficient in the original language of the materials. Additionally, vector databases can be utilized to store multilingual word embeddings, enabling efficient language mapping and improved translation quality.

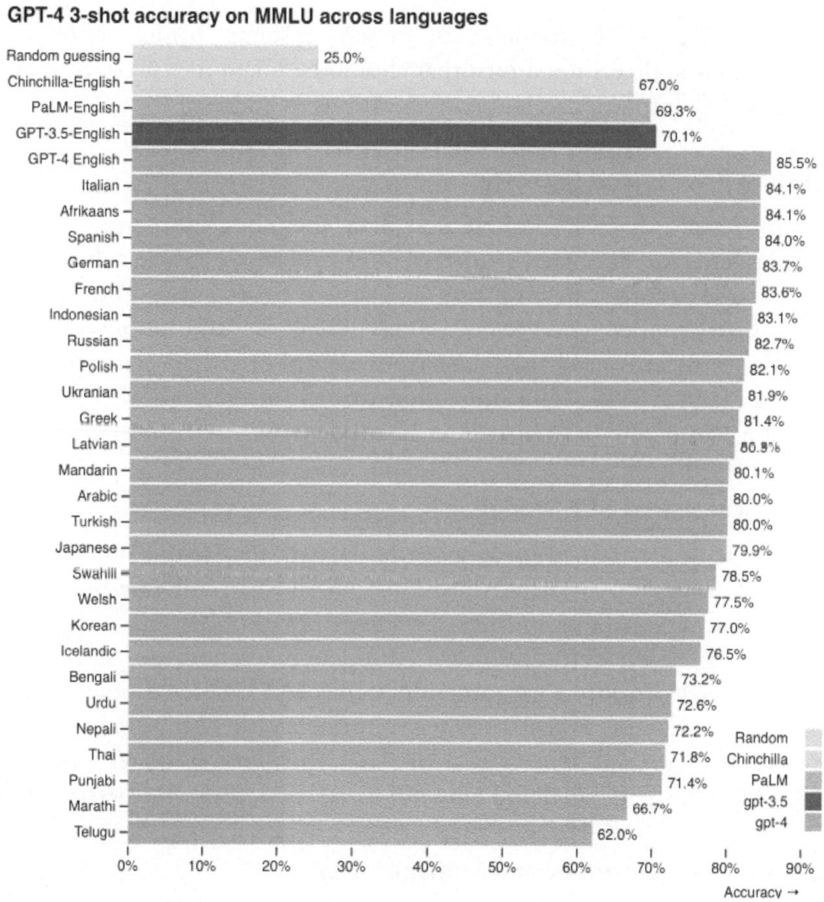


**Figure 2**

*The above figure from the GPT-4 Technical Report published by OpenAI shows its 3-shot accuracy on MMLU across languages.*

In these applications, the data collected from library catalogues, user interactions, and other relevant sources is used to train the GPT models and develop algorithms specific to each application. Additionally, vector databases are utilized to store and retrieve vector representations of library resources and user preferences, enabling efficient similarity matching and enhancing the accuracy and effectiveness of the GPT-based functionalities in library systems.

## IMPLICATIONS AND CONSIDERATIONS

Implementing GPT models in library systems brings numerous implications and considerations that should be taken into account. Here are some key implications and considerations to address:

### (a) Data Privacy and Security

Library systems handle sensitive user data, including borrowing history, user preferences, and search queries. It is crucial to ensure robust data privacy and security measures are in place to protect user information. Implement proper encryption, access controls, and anonymization techniques to safeguard user data from unauthorized access or misuse. Comply with relevant data protection regulations and adhere to ethical guidelines to maintain user trust and confidentiality.

### (b) Ethical Use of GPT Models

GPT models are trained on large-scale datasets that may contain biases or reflect societal prejudices. Care must be taken to mitigate biases and ensure fairness in the outputs generated by GPT models. Regular monitoring, bias detection, and mitigation techniques should be implemented to address any potential biases and ensure equitable access to library resources. Transparently communicate the limitations of GPT models to users, highlighting that the recommendations or responses are algorithmically generated and may not always reflect diverse perspectives.

### (c) User Empowerment and Transparency

Library users should have control over the recommendations they receive and be able to understand how the GPT models operate. Provide users with options to customize or fine-tune the recommendations according to their preferences. Clearly communicate to users that GPT models are used to improve recommendations, virtual assistant interactions, or other functionalities, and provide mechanisms for users to provide feedback or report any issues encountered.

### (d) Continuous Evaluation and Improvement

Regularly evaluate the performance and effectiveness of GPT models in library systems. Monitor user satisfaction, recommendation accuracy, response quality, and other relevant metrics to identify areas for improvement. Incorporate user feedback and iteratively refine the implementation to enhance the user experience and address any shortcomings or limitations of the GPT models.

### (e) Human Oversight and Collaboration

While GPT models offer powerful capabilities, human oversight and collaboration remain essential. Ensure that trained library staff are available to address user queries, provide additional assistance, or validate the outputs generated by GPT models. Human expertise and judgment play a vital role in maintaining the quality and integrity of the library services and resources.

### (f) Accessibility and Inclusivity

Consider the accessibility needs of diverse user groups, including individuals with visual impairments, language barriers, or other disabilities. Ensure that GPT-based functionalities, such as virtual assistants or figure descriptions, are accessible and provide alternative means of accessing information for users with different needs. Follow accessibility standards and guidelines to make library services inclusive and accessible to all.

### (g) Resource Allocation and Scalability

GPT models require significant computational resources, including processing power and storage, for training and deployment. Consider the resource requirements and scalability of the infrastructure to accommodate the computational demands of GPT models. Optimize resource allocation and explore cloud-based solutions for distributed computing options to effectively scale the implementation as the library system grows.

## CONCLUSION

The integration of GPT models into library systems represents an exciting advancement that holds significant potential. These models, which have been trained on vast amounts of text data, offer promising applications such as personalized recommendations, virtual assistants, language translation, figure and image description, and text summary-zation. By leveraging GPT models, libraries can enhance user experiences, improve accessibility, and cater to the evolving needs of readers.

However, the implementation of GPT models in library systems requires careful consideration of various implications and considerations. Safeguarding user privacy and data security, addressing biases, ensuring transparency, and maintaining human oversight are essential aspects to uphold ethical standards. Continuous evaluation, user feedback, and collaboration with trained library staff are vital for refining the performance of GPT models and providing the highest quality services to library users.

Furthermore, accessibility and inclusivity should be at the forefront of the implementation process. By catering to diverse user groups and adhering to accessibility standards, libraries can ensure that GPT-based functionalities are accessible to all, regardless of language barriers or disabilities.

As libraries embrace GPT models, it is important to strike a balance between the power of technology and the human touch. Human expertise and judgment continue to play a crucial role in maintaining the integrity of library resources and services, while GPT models augment and enhance user experiences.

In conclusion, the incorporation of GPT models into library systems presents a compelling opportunity to revolutionize library services. By utilizing these models, libraries can provide personalized recommendations, interactive virtual assistants, multilingual access, improved image description, and efficient text summarization. However, it is crucial to carefully consider the associated implications and considerations, such as data privacy, bias detection, and user transparency. By striking a balance between technological advancements and human expertise, libraries can create a dynamic and inclusive environment that enhances the user experience and promotes learning in the digital era.

## REFERENCES

[1] Open AI (2023, March 15). GPT-4 Technical Report. arXiv.org. https://arxiv.org/abs/2303.08774

[2] Brown, T.B. (2020, May 28). Language Models are Few-Shot Learners. arXiv.org. https://arxiv.org/abs/2005.14165

[3] Radford, A. and Narasimhan, K. (2018). Improving Language Understanding by Generative Pre-Training.

# Online Versus Traditional Libraries

**Satish Kumar***

**Abstract**

In this paper we are discussion between online and traditional libraries in a holistic ways of libraries. In addition to storing content, digital libraries provide a way to organize search and retrieve the contents of a collection whereas traditional libraries emphasize the archive and preservation of physical items especially books and periodicals that were the custodians of the librarian library.

A digital library, also called an online library, an internet library, a digital repository, or a digital collection is an online database of digital objects that can include text, still images, audio, video, digital document or other digital media formats or a library accessible through the internet.

This paper is focusing digital/online library, e-library resource advantages, challenges and disadvantage.

*Keywords: Online Library, Digital Library, Internet.*

**Characteristic of online library and traditional library:** Online library has certain characteristics, which makes them different from traditional library. It has expansive and accurate system of searching with large volume of text, image and audio video resources. Digital libraries do not need physical space to build collection and it can be accessed from any where any time.

## Salient Feature of Online Library

| | | |
|---|---|---|
| Resource of information | - | Virtual |
| Storing type | - | Electronic |
| Acquisition | - | Online |
| Cataloging | - | Not available |

---

*

Accessing - Online
Preservation - Electronic
Storage - Digital repositories

### Traditional Library

Physical searching method is using to retrieve the resources. Information is stored in physical format. The users may borrowed the resources and make use of it a traditional library consist details of availed stock in books and subscription of periodicals.

### Salient Features of Traditional Library

Resources of information - Physical
Storing type - Printed
Acquisition - Traditional
Cataloging - Traditional
Accessing - By hand/automated
Preservation - Traditional
Storage - Traditional Repositories

### Advantages of Digital Library

Digital libraries can range in size and scope and they can be maintained by individuals, organizations or established physical library buildings or institution affiliated with approved or academic institutions.

As we cleared this on up we will introduce you to the advantage of digital library:

1. Wide variety of content available
2. Easily updated
3. On demand access
4. Simplified search
5. 24*7 availability
6. Unlimited access to multiple resources
7. Library management automation
8. Real time interactions
9. Reduce resource depletion
10. Preserving knowledge for future Generations

## Advantage or Traditional Library

There is a lot of advantage while using traditional library resources. Because it is some features like the format size, quality and easy to handling.

1. Traditional print resources are able to read even if computer are failure.
2. Users can turn the pages comfortably the traditional print resources. Because of the familiarity.
3. There is no need of any technology for read the print resources.
4. User can spend long time for using print resource.
5. A traditional format of prints resources is more portable, easier to read and better to handle.
6. Traditional printed resources remain readable for many years.
7. Printed resources are environmental.
8. The printed resources are not creating any pollution in the environment.

## Challenges with Digital Library

Some important problems and challenges associated with digital libraries are following:

1. Information accuracy
2. Compatibility of hardware/software
3. Reliability of information
4. IPR issues (intellectual property right)
5. Data security
6. Fair use
7. Convenience of usage
8. Needs Technology
9. Costly
10. Shelf life/storage life
11. Digital reading and storage devices should be Omni present

## Digital Resources: User Priorities

1. OPAC
2. Data bases
3. E-journals
4. E-book
5. Audio visual
6. Dissertations
7. Online reports
8. Online standards

## Disadvantages of Traditional Library Resources

1. If users want traditional print resources he/she should visit the library during the working hours only.
2. Only one user can use printed resources at one time.
3. Maximum number of printed reference books is available at I price even there are number of free search engines and search directories for user reference purpose.

## Difference between Traditional and Digital Library

1. **Traditional Library:** Library staff perform their duties in the acquisition section, cataloging section, classification section, periodical section as well as different sections as per requirement.

2. To wire books, periodicals, journals, proper vendors and as recommended by users and the management authority.
3. To record properly acquired resources both print and digital.
4. To provide in abstracting, indexing, information.
5. To provide information from the traditional source including access to digital resources.

### Digital Library

1. To provide easy access to information to users available in various electronics format.
2. To procure eBooks and online journals and other digital publications to the users as per needs.
3. To develop library website for getting information from different location by giving links to resources.
4. To provide access to back issues of online journals to the users.
5. Learn skill to mountain the digital library in addition to technical

## CONCLUSION

Based on the facts of challenges and advantage and disadvantages with traditional and online library written above, we can say that online library cannot replace the traditional library because both types of library have their own importance in a meaningful way, as in the present the importance of online library is more visible in time, then the history of traditional library has also been very old and rich.

The historical sources of traditional libraries date back to 6000 years ago when humans used to store their records their ideas through pictorial script Silk, leather, and tapes etc.

Other sources such as used to papyrus in Egypt as a writing aid during 3000 BC and Palm leaf manuscript was also used in the traditional library in the early stage is just like the early stages in the online library now in OPAC and MARC moving to RFID and wide digitalization of automation has taken the form of digitalization has held and is presenting a model to demonstrate the concept of a comprehensive digitalization.

Thus the existence of both traditional and online libraries has been inter related, it would not be an exaggeration.

# Impact of Information and Communication Technology (ICT) in Libraries of Technical Institutions in Present Times

**Abhishek Kumar Sharma[1], Annu Sharma[2], Pradeep Kapurwan[3] and Umang Bansal[4]**

## Abstract

Information and Communication Technology (ICT) is playing an important role in bringing many changes in our lives. Human life is unimaginable without information and communication technology. In today's time, the researcher has to search for his deprived information by using information and communication technology in many ways throughout the day. Without information and communication technology, no researcher can access the desired information. At present, as technology is becoming more advanced and easily available every day, the quality of services provided by libraries also increases. In this era of ICT, the role of educational, public, medical, defense, agriculture etc. libraries has completely changed in developed countries, for this reason libraries of any field are providing accurate and precise information and services to their users. But due to lack of funds in many places, information and communication technology is not being developed in libraries, due to which users have to depend on many other types of resources. As a result the users of public libraries in developing countries are not fully satisfied. This paper deals with the development of educational institute libraries located in Dehradun, their present status and some important works for improving their services and implementing ICT.(1) 1

[1] Research Scholar of Himalayiya University Librarian, Tula's Institute Dehradun, India. E-mail: sr.librarian@tulas.edu.in

[2] Research Scholar, Himalayiya University, Librarian, Himalayiya Ayurdic Medical P.G College, Dehradun, India. E-mail: annu_sharma17@rediffmail.com

[3] Research Scholar of Himalayiya University, Assistant Librarian of DIT University, Dehradun, India. E-mail: pkapruwan110@gmail.com

[4] Library Technical Assistant, IIT, Roorkee, India.
E-mail: Umangbansallib1979@gmail.com

***Keywords:*** *Information and Communication Technology, Library, Educational Institute, University Libraries, Dehradun.*

## INTRODUCTION

In present times, due to the increasing influence of information and communication technology, different types of technologies are being used for different types of services provided in the library. In this era of information and communication technology new developments are taking place every day which are affecting the way libraries work and provide information. Due to the increasing influence of information and communication technology in libraries, it is necessary for library workers and librarians to have knowledge about new information technology and communication technology useful for the library. There can be different types of users in any library, such as researchers, institute officials, teachers, undergraduate and postgraduate students, etc., whosc information needs are of different types, which are solved by different types of information. This can be done only by using the resources of technology and communication technology. (2) 2 From the point of view of information and communication technology, computerized library management has become the most important technology among various ICT applications used by developing countries for the last several years to meet all kinds of information needs of researchers, research institutes and others. types of users in all developing countries. I am capable we can also define computerized libraries in such a way that computerized libraries emphasize on the use of various sources of information technology and communication technology used for information storage and re-use of such information., Information technology and communication technology are seen as the catalyst of economic, material, social and educational development of any country in today's time, because without the use of information technology and communication technology, no country can develop from a developing country today. It is possible the country cannot complete the path of being. Information technology and communication technology are not essential but necessary to raise awareness. (3) 3 Information technology and communication technology are important tools in libraries for managing and storing information. No library can achieve its goal without adopting information technology and communication technology, because Communication technology has completely changed the format, means and way of working of libraries related to academic, scientific, agricultural, defense etc. In today's time, no institution can be imagined without information technology and communication technology. In today's time, information technology and communication technology have emerged as an integral part of any institute and library. (4) 4 The term ICT is used to describe a range of devices such as hardware, software, personal computers, scanners, mobile phones, printers, barcode scanners, etc.

## ICT RESOURCES AND SERVICES IN PRIVATE UNIVERSITY LIBRARIES OF DEHRADUN DISTRICT, UTTARAKHAND

The development and availability of Information and Communication Technology (ICT) in the present times has not only accelerated and disseminated the use of information resources in libraries today but has also placed greater emphasis on effective and efficient Information and Communication Technology services. The application of information and communication technology (ICT) in libraries, commonly known as library automation and quick, timely access and transfer of information resources is an important factor, simple and important. The importance of various information and communication technology services provided in libraries has been appreciated by the users from time to time. (4) 5

Dehradun district of Uttarakhand has made a lot of progress in the field of higher education in the 21st century, and has given higher education a new height. At present, there are many non-government and government universities in Dehradun, which are making important contribution in the field of education; communication technology (ICT) centers have been built in all universities to promote education. The use of information communication technology (ICT) in libraries has become more widespread than before. Various types of communication technology (ICT) tools are being used by the library to search the missing information of the researcher.

In most libraries, advanced software is used for entry of books like LIBSYS, KOHA, Soul etc. Book distribution, barcode, e-journals, e-books are being used by the libraries for the students. In present times it would be futile to imagine any library without a Communication Technology (ICT) centre. There are more options available for researchers to get their information than ever before, due to which if libraries do not use information communication technology (ICT) in their functioning, the importance of libraries will end for researchers. In today's era, every student has personal mobile and internet facility, using which he can get his deprived information.

At present, libraries should not only open communication technology (ICT) centers, but also observe from time to time whether the equipment, e-resources, software etc. available in the center are being used properly or not, if not, then what steps should be taken by the library so that all the resources can be used properly and completely, it should also be contemplated.

All the libraries should also take steps whether the Information Technology (ICT) Center available in their library can also benefit the students of other institutions where Information Technology (ICT) Center is not available.

## FOR PROPER FUNCTIONING OF ANY LIBRARY THERE ARE SOME ICT FACILITIES OR RESOURCES WHICH CAN BE USED

- **Library Software Services:** The library should provide its users with the facility to issue and deposit books from the library software. The account of the books issued by the software remains safe in the software for a long time, so that in case of any dispute, the dispute can be easily resolved by the library.
- **Library Repository:** An online repository should be created by the library for its users, with the help of which any user can get their deprived study material like old question papers, old research papers etc.
- **Library CAS & SDI Services:** Library CAS and SDI Services refers to the facilities provided by the library to the users, such as providing information about new books coming to the library, important information coming in the newspaper, information about research papers, etc.
- **Library Email, FAX and Chat services:** From time to time, the availability of new old resources of the library by the library to its users by e-mail, fax or chatting apps, what new services have been started in the library, any user has access to the library Giving information about what resources are available, etc. is included.
- **E-Resource Database:** Which databases are taken by the library for the users and how the database helps the users in searching the desired information, giving information to the users through e-mail, fax, chat etc.

- **Providing printing, reprographic and scanning services to the users by the library:** Providing printing, reprographic and scanning etc. services to the users by the library: The library should create a reprographic section in the library, in which the facility of print, photo state, scanning etc. should be provided for the users, which saves the time and money of the users and Dr. S.R. Ranganathan's 4th Laws are meaningful.
- **OPAC and SMS Services:** The library should provide facility to the users to communicate with each other (Online Public Access Code), so that the information about the resources available in the library will be available to the students from time to time without spending time. The library should also have the facility of SMS service for the students, so that the students can get the information about the books issued and deposited in the library through SMS on the phone and any kind of trouble can be avoided in the future.
- **Online Facility of E-books, E-journals and Dissertations for the Students by the Library:** There should be arrangement of e-books, e-journals, dissertation and thesis etc. for the students in the library so that the students do not have to go anywhere other than the library. Whatever type of study material is needed by the students, whether that material is available in the library or not, it includes the services of finding and bringing it for the students.
- **Plagiarism Software Services:** The library should provide the facility of Plagiarism software service for its users to know the correctness of the research done by them, so that any user can check the correctness of his research paper and make corrections in case of error.
- **Facilitating the Exchange of Resources:** Knowing the interests of its users, the library should talk to other libraries about the exchange of resources, so that duplication of resources in the library can be avoided and more resource users can get more resources by spending less money can be done.
- **Internet and Wi-Fi Services:** The library should arrange internet for its users in the computer lab, along with it should be mandatory for the students who work on their mobiles and laptops to make proper arrangements for Wi-Fi and charging points in the library.
- **Library Portal or Library Website Service:** The librarian should ensure that it should be mandatory to have a library portal on the

website of the institute and also the library portal should have all the information related to the library. The librarian should also ensure that if possible, the library has its own website, in which the librarian can give information about all the services of his library, as well as the information about the program can reach all the users by putting the program in the library on the website.

- **NPTEL, Swayam, Moocs, and NDLI Services:** The Library Department should provide information to its users about Moocs courses through SWAYAM portal from time to time. NPTEL videos should be presented in the library from time to time for the users.
- **Open Source Software Services:** The library should appoint an employee in the library department for its users, who can provide information about the open source software used by the users and help them to run the software.
- **RFID Services:** Radio Frequency Identification Service is the latest technology in libraries, using which the theft of library material can be prevented. Radio frequency identification system uses techniques that use radio waves, through which it has become easier and faster to identify library materials. It's easy to track and manage content and automatically across libraries.

## ADVANTAGE OF USING INFORMATION AND COMMUNICATION TECHNOLOGY (ICT) RELATED TECHNIQUES AND TOOLS IN LIBRARIES OF TECHNICAL EDUCATIONAL INSTITUTIONS

Organizing the mediums of information and communication is an essential and primary activity. Due to the expansion and dissemination of information through information and communication, the tools of information and communication. Many studies done in the past have directly described the importance of ICT facilities, in which the savings of facilities and time for the researcher due to ICT for library operations is very important. ICT especially has the potential to provide more and faster facilities with less money than the traditional library system. (5) 6 Ogunsola (2004) in his study found that the use of ICT has had a significant impact on human life and their living conditions. Many revolutionary changes have been seen on human life with the use of ICT. With the use of ICT, everyone has easy access to information about the country and abroad or information related to any field. (6) 7 ICT has changed information science and information communication. Old equipment and techniques have been replaced by modern equipment, where earlier half the space was required to keep library material, after the use of ICT, that deficiency has also been completed because it is easier to keep e-books than hard books. This does not take up space at all. Databases are replacing huge Chisenga (1999), ICT in libraries has changed the way information is accessed. Of news storage and retrieval, acquisition, cataloging and classification, movement of materials, serial control, management statistics and administrative activities like budgeting etc. have been greatly simplified. (7) **8** ICT helps in keeping pace with the latest developments in the day-to-day work of the library, with the help of various technologies incorporated in it, many types of tasks can be easily accomplished like sending mail to someone, which earlier was done through correspondence. Used to be from ICT includes many types of services such as IRC, e-mail of the Internet, etc.). (8) **9**

- **Easy to Use:** The use of ICT by the library saves the time of both the user and the library personnel, such as applying barcodes on books, we can scan the barcode with a scanner and give the book to the user without losing time, there are many libraries software's in the market for automation. There are types of library software available through which we can convert our library from manual to automated library, by which we can save the time of library users and library personnel. ICT is very easy to use for the users of the library. Many libraries are appointing ICT experts in their library especially for ICT center which has made it very easy for the library users to use ICT tools in the library.
- **Open Source Learning Platform:** At present, there are many types of open source platforms available which are easily available to the users without spending any money. By using which any user can join any seminar, workshop, online course etc. in any country, due to which there is saving of time as well as money. Swayam, Moocs etc. are one type of online learning course platforms which are working to provide education to the users sitting at home without asking for just some amount of money. Users can improve their ICT skills by using all these types of sources.
- **Free Online Tools:** Keeping in mind the importance of ICT, software companies of many countries have launched many types of free mobile learning apps in the market, such as doc scanner, file converter, image editor, etc., using which any user can download the app according to their own needs. Could get help to do your

work easily without spending any money. There are many types of software available in the market which cannot come in the budget of every user, online platform is a convenient way to solve this problem, from where users by installing many types of free software, you can easily complete your work.

- **Save Money, Time and Space:** By using ICT, many libraries are currently working on reducing the time and cost of other libraries by sharing their library resources with other libraries, thereby saving their time and money. For example DELNET platform is a convenient platform in which we can access the resources of many other member libraries by subscribing to DELNET by paying a minimal fee, we can request any type of article, book and other text from DELNET. By USE all these types of platforms and other online software, we can also save the space of the library because physical books occupy a lot of space whereas only system and software are needed to keep online books. (9) **10**
- **ICT for use:** At present, every library has the right to use ICT technology and tools to develop their own and their library users' skills. With the use of ICT, there will be many changes in the society, due to which there will be personal development of human beings as well as the development of the country.

## VARIOUS PROBLEMS FACED BY THE NON-AUTOMATED LIBRARY SERVICE SYSTEM LOCATED IN DEHRADUN

Effective library services at present depend to an extent on information and communication technology, but the integration of ICT for library service delivery presents enormous challenges and opportunities. For the increasing information needs of the library, there is a need for expansion of information technology tools in the library on a large scale. The educational and research needs of library users make it difficult for any library to be an effective learning resource. Nowadays, without the use of modern IT facilities, no academic library can function effectively, prosper or achieve the desired library objectives. For the use of IT, it has become necessary to establish an IT center in the library department because the prosperity of any library is due to its IT center and IT equipment. Only having an IT center in the library will not work, for this the librarian will also have to make arrangements for trained IT staff in the library. (12) **10** In present time's lot of efforts have been made to streamline library services and operations from manual process to adoption of IT solutions. It is very unfortunate that till now many academic libraries have not been able to achieve their desired goal even after the establishment of IT center. In libraries, we can basically divide the goals into two categories, first automatic and second non-automatic goals. To make a clear distinction between the challenges, we classify the libraries into two. First automated libraries means completely IT driven library and non-automated library means completely run by library personnel. (13) **11**

- **Unawareness of New Technologies Used in the Library from Time to Time:** The staffs of libraries running without the use of ICT lack the use of ICT, due to which they lag behind other ICT-using library personnel. This stunts their personal, professional and library development. Without the use of ICT, no library can be able to find or make available to its users the information they lack.
- **Time Consuming:** Working in the library is a difficult task since ancient times, due to which in the present time, if ICT is not used by the libraries for the convenience of the students, then the student will have difficulty in getting his deprived information or it may also happen. is that students may not be able to succeed even after spending a lot of time searching for the missing information.

## DISADVANTAGE OF USING INFORMATION AND COMMUNICATION TECHNOLOGY (ICT) RELATED TECHNIQUES AND TOOLS IN LIBRARIES OF TECHNICAL EDUCATIONAL INSTITUTIONS

At present, every library has to go through many types of difficulties, in which there are many types of factors which reduce the use of ICT in the library, in which the main factor is the lack of time, difficulties in using ICT. The need for assistance and training, new technologies coming in the market everyday and lack of skilled workers in the library, etc. E-learning can increase the learning speed of users and simplify the learning process; however, many restrictions have been imposed on ICT training due to a variety of problems, which slow down the speed of training. In which the lack of money can also be considered as the main factor. No library can serve its understanding and users until the library is provided with adequate funds for the desired material. Thus, due to many reasons, there has been a big lack in the use of ICT in the library. (2) **11**

- **High cost of e-resources and limited budget of the library:** Use of ICT in library is not an easy task because in present time the cost of e-resources is very high. Every institution is not able to take every type of e-resource because a library needs many types of resources to function which include books, hard journals, furniture's, library repository, skilled workers etc. Is unable to purchase any type of resource. A limited budget is issued by any institution to its library, out of which the library has to meet all its needs, due to which many times the library is left behind in the field of ICT. (2) **12**
- **Difficulties in using e-resources:** Libraries must review their resources from time to time to keep themselves updated. There are many types of technologies used in the library, which keep getting updated day by day, due to which it is a challenging task for library staff and library users to always use ICT correctly. It is important for the library to transmit information about the new technologies available in the library from time to time to its employees and its users through any resource. (10) **13**
- **Lack of ICT skilled workers in the library:** At present, new resources of ICT in the library are developing rapidly in the market every day, due to which the library departments are struggling with the shortage of skilled workers. ICT operated library has to deal with many types of technical tasks, in which knowledge of operating many types of equipment, which new techniques are necessary for library improvement, it is difficult for library personnel to have knowledge of software, hardware etc. It has happened, due to which the library needs skilled librarians on a daily basis. (11) **14**

## CONCLUSION

Library is an important means for the dissemination of knowledge in the society, which is formed by many types of resources and gives knowledge to the people living in the society about the importance of education and the objectives of their life. In present times, librarians and library personnel should inform their users about the importance of library and all kinds of resources available in the library. Many times the information sought by the users is not necessarily available in the library, but the library should create such a library network that any type of resource or information should reach the users. Librarians should understand the information and resource needs of their users and fulfill their desired needs as far as possible. It should be ensured in the library that every type of resources available in the library should be properly and fully utilized. If the library does not work only for the users of the institution, it should also work in the society around it, so it should be ensured that no one remains without knowledge, because the main function/purpose of the library is to increase the knowledge of the users and Along with this, there is also an increase in the knowledge of the society. If the library is able to achieve its intended objectives, then it can be said that the services available in the library are excellent. The success of any library depends on the library worker, the material available in the library and the technology used by the library, if ICT is being used in the library and ICT is being used properly and fully, then one day No person will be able to be illiterate in the society.

## REFERENCES


[1] Shuva, Nafiz Zaman. "Implementing information and communication technology in public libraries of Bangladesh." *The International information & library review,* 37, No. 3 (2005): 159–168.

[2] Krubu, Dorcas Ejemeh and Kingsley Efe Osawaru. "The impact of information and communication technology (ICT) in Nigerian university libraries." *Library philosophy and Practice*, 2011, No. 583 (2011): 1–19.

[3] Park, Namkee, Raul Roman, Seungyoon Lee and Jae Eun Chung. "User acceptance of a digital library system in developing countries: An application of the Technology Acceptance Model." *International journal of information management,* 29, No. 3 (2009): 196–209.

[4] Mishra, Lakshmikant, and Jyoti Mishra. "ICT resources and services in university libraries." International Journal of Digital Library Services, 4, No. 3 (2014): 243–250.

[5] Ajemasu, Madalla, Yusuf Mohammed Inuwa, Yusuf Saad and Abdullshi Adamu Jumba. "Information and Communication Technology (ICT) in libraries: A new dimension in librarianship." (2019).

[6] Chisenga, J. (2004). ICT in Libraries: An overview and general.

[7] Ajemasu, Madalla, Yusuf Mohammed Inuwa, Yusuf Saad, and Abdullshi Adamu Jumba. "Information and Communication Technology (ICT) in libraries: A new dimension in librarianship" (2019).

[8] Ratheeswari, K. "Information communication technology in education." *Journal of Applied and Advanced research 3*, No. 1 (2018): 45–47.

[9] Madalla Ajemasu *et al.* (2019).

[10] Saleem, A., T.S.Z. Shabana and M. Sadik Batcha. "Application and uses of Information Communication Technology (ICT) in academic libraries:

an overview." *International Journal of Library Science,* 2, No. 3 (2013): 49–52.

[11] Abdelrahman, Omer Hassan. "The state of ICT implementation and training at the University of Khartoum library system (UKLIS)." *ICAL2009–Vision and roles of the future academic libraries* (2009).

[12] Haruna Abdu, Abubakar Aliyu, Umeh Paulinus and Mubarak Umar. "The Integration of cloud computing technology in academic library operations towards effective library services." *Integration,* 3, No. 1 (2017): 82–88.

[13] Solutions., In present times lot of efforts have been made to streamline library services and operations from manual process to adoption of IT.

[14] Talebian, Sogol, Hamid Movahed Mohammadi, and Ahmad Rezvanfar. "Information and communication technology (ICT) in higher education: Advantages, disadvantages, conveniences and limitations of applying e-learning to agricultural students in Iran." *Procedia.*

[15] Ogunsola, L.A. and W.A. Aboyade. "Information and communication technology in Nigeria: Revolution or evolution." *Journal of Social Sciences,* 11, No. 1 (2005): 7–14.

[16] Krubu, Dorcas Ejemeh and Kingsley Efe Osawaru. "The impact of information and communication technology (ICT) in Nigerian university libraries." *Library philosophy and Practice,* 2011, No. 583 (2011): 1–19.

# Knowledge Management and New Generation of Library Information

**Punita Sharma***

**Abstract**

The Library will play a very crucial role in the extension and modification of knowledge. The growing need for knowledge management has influenced every component and operation of a library. Knowledge management requires more effective methods of information handling, speedy transfer of information and linking of information with individuals and their activity. Knowledge management is a newly emerging interdisciplinary business model that has knowledge with the frame work of an organization. Knowledge management involves people technology and processes in parts, it rests on two foundations first utilizing and exploiting the organization information, second the application of people's skill, talents thought, ideas, commitments, motivations and imagination. The advancement of information communication technology ICT most of the sources and reading material are available in electronic format which can be access through online and offline both. Electronic resources are becoming popular due to technology changes and advancement now in present scenario we are able to get electronic- resources management across the word within few movements. Electronic resources management are becoming more popular due to its easy access and time saving. Due to enormous growth and continuous development of Technology the role of library.

***Keywords:*** *Knowledge Management In Library, Types of Knowledge Management, Module of Knowledge Management, ICT in Library, Objective of ICT, Library and Information Profession, Electronic Resources Management, Types of Electronic Resources, Objective of Electronic Resources Management System.*

* Assistant Professor, Chaman Lal Mahavidyalaya, Landhaura, Haridwar, India. E-mail: punitasharma1977@gmail.com

## INTRODUCTION

Knowledge play and important role in modern world of organization knowledge management was started and popular in the business word during the last decade of the 20 century. It was the business word that first recognize the important of knowledge in the "Global economy" of knowledge" As a subject discipline of the knowledge economy, knowledge management is completely new concept and method of Management. Knowledge management is very essential to the success of the organization as it not only help is discovering the resources but in the newly scenario also help in evolving new business rule and models. When we refer to knowledge, most of use mainly trend to think of codified and documented knowledge like patents database manual, white paper etc. There is no Universal Definition of knowledge management, 10 as there is no agreement as to what constitute knowledge in the first place. For this reason it is best to think of knowledge management in the broadest contest knowledge management is the process through which organization generate value from there intellectual knowledge base asset. Most often comma generating value from such asset involve sharing them among employees departments and even with other company in and effort to device best practice full stop it is important to note that the definition say nothing about technology. While knowledge management is often facilitated by information technology by itself is not knowledge management.

## KNOWLEDGE MANAGEMENT IN LIBRARY

Information technology is a tool for knowledge management in library knowledge acquisition is the starting point of knowledge management in library. The application of information technology in large the scope of knowledge acquisition. The objective of knowledge management of library is to promote knowledge innovation. Knowledge innovation is the core of the knowledge economy society. As base for collection storage and distribution of knowledge and information. Library represent and indispensable link in the scientific system Chain and important link in the knowledge innovation secondly library take part in scientific research process directly. The library work is a component of knowledge innovation. Hardly library must per attention to diffusion and conversion of knowledge full stop knowledge management in library is to promote relationship in library between libraries and user, to strength knowledge Internet working and quicken knowledge flow. In the knowledge economy era library will carry out research on development and application of information resources construction of virtual library, protection of intellectual property rights in the electronic era etc, does pounding the base for knowledge innovation.

## MODULE OF KNOWLEDGE MANAGEMENT

The KM system is primary base on seven vital modules. These modules are:

1. Information
2. Expertise
3. Collaboration
4. Team
5. Learning
6. Intelligence
7. Knowledge transfer

## ICT IN LIBRARY

The information communication technology has made a tremendous improvement and change almost all work of life. It play significant role in optimum use of library resources. ICT is concerned with the storage, retrieval, manipulation, transmission or receipt of digital data. With the advent of smart phone and other latest ICT tools and gadget the formation of information as well as its dissemination has change drastically. Today's library or not merely a collection of books but they have Transform into pollution of useful material in print electronic multimedia and all other possible format librarian/information professionals are facing challenges as the today's Clinton is more Technology oriented and they need the information immediately on the desktop slash palmtop or smart phones or whatever mode/device of communication they are using and feel convenient. As the user are the ultimate beneficiary of services of the library in any kind of academic dash resource Institute and their satisfaction is prime is prime objective of librarian also user are the customers to the library services seems the changing in information needs of the library services. Seeing the changing in information needs of the library users in challenging format is creating a constant pressure on the library information professionals to update them regularly and keep them aware of latest trends.

## OBJECTIVE OF ICT

To provide greater and easier excess information second point to allow access to computers and the internet for everybody so that a device does not build a between those who do not poses computer to access people to develop their ICT skills for accessing the information to give access to digital learning materials which are set to increase in both quality and quantity to provide staff expertise to sick out information or leaving material staff become killed gatekeepers not just stop printed sources but of the digitized once too.

## LIBRARY AND INFORMATION PROFESSION

As per ALA world Encyclopedia of Information and Library service says maintenance of knowledge growth in skin and the development of competence of performing rules in the work environment are critical aspect of a profession the library professionals have to develop skills to cope with the change their skills of classification cataloguing, indexing etc. are to be remolded for data analysis data structuring, data organization packaging and Re Packaging of Information and for providing value added library and information services the basis and fundamental of librarian skill to provide right information to the right uses at the right time are not going to be changed in the digital library environment in spite of the various barriers in the skill development lie economic, psychological, culture social and political barriers and barriers of existing information Infrastructures the librarian will acquire tightly still and continue to be a reliable source for information seekers the technology for the electronic transfer of information is developing rapidly we are now moving towards paper lies information the includes the digitization of information, drawings etc. their electronic transmission electronic ordering, payment extra. Education and training of library profession and user has become the major issue to cough with the new environment. Library information science education has to adopt multimedia approach in importing knowledge and skills to stop National teaching method should be replaced by newer educational media. Educational potential of the computer and its versatility has to be fully released. Computer Aided instructions(CAI) and Computer Aided learning (CAL) have to be incorporated to understand the concept the library Academy must broader beyond the home front two become International in school. Training and development opportunities for librarian and user for optimal and utilization of digital innovation a to be encouraged and revitalized NISSAT, NICNET, C-DOT, ERNET and other leading national bodies should regularly organize the training programs for the library professionals.

## Electronic Resources Management

Electronic resources management system represent and increasingly important component of the collection building activity of academic and public library. Electronic resources management system (ERMS) refer to those materials that require computer access, whether through personal computer, mainframe handled mobile device, As the number and method of accessing electronic products have increased, the management of these resources has become more complex. Prior to electronic resources management system electronic resources management stored information in a variety of place and format. In house database, spreadsheets, email and paper file were used to store subscription details password, vendor contact information licence agreement. Unfortunately in many situation very few library staff has access to that data. The source which are available in electronic formats now as E-resources such as E-books E-journals, E-newspaper, E-magazine, databases Bibliography databases etc. Due to the advancement of information communication technology ICT most of the sources and reading material are available in electronic format which can be access through online and offline both. Electronic resources are becoming popular due to technology changes and advancement now in present scenario we are able to get electronic-resources management across the word within few movements. Electronic resources management are becoming more popular due to its easy access and time saving. Due to enormous growth and continuous development of Technology the role of library become more responsive in making the user technology. Technological development have affected not only the formats and sources of information but also how and where to provide library services.

## TYPES OF ELECTRONIC RESOURCES

The electronic resources are basically divided in various major type are: E-books; E-general; E-database; Website; CD ROM; Hard Disk; Diskettes; Other Portable Device.

## OBJECTIVE OF ELECTRONIC RESOURCES MANAGEMENT SYSTEM

Electronic resources management system becoming very popular and Library users are satisfied with it. Libraries are including maximum e-resources in its collections. Main objective of resources are:

Development of the library: An electronic resource participates for the development of the library. Today rich collection of the library is becoming base of the library because which library is more and more electronic resources oriented that library called resourcefulness which library include maximum electronic resources within its profit that library can complete with other libraries.

## CURRENT AND UPDATED INFORMATION

Main task of electronic resources is to provide Maximum current and updated information for its users. Which library subscribe maximum electronics resources that Users Research Scholars and Faculty of that institution is attached with current and updated information and targets of that institution is achieved save the time electronic resources save the time of the staff as well as users. In printed and big collection time of the staff and user was more spend, but in electronic mode it can be easily accessed.

### Space Problem

Electronic resources solve the space problem. Printed collection required more space than electronic resources.

## INCREASE IN NUMBER OF USERS

Electronic resources promote services of the library. In electronic environment library users are spending more time within the libraries. They can easily access required information or document within time and its promotes quantity and quality of the users within the library.

## COOPERATIVE AND RESOURCES SHARING

Electronic resources becoming role model for promoting corporation and resources sharing between libraries. Through networking electronic resources can be shared between library. Two or more libraries collaboratively purchase and share different electronic resources for their libraries.

Users Satisfactions: In information explosion era every library wants to purchase those resources which are beneficial for its users therefore electronic resources which are beneficial for its users therefore electronic resources are also available online and libraries can and decide which electronic resources are beneficial for its users and its satisfactions.

## CONCULSION

Knowledge Management is not owned by any one group in an organization, nor by any one profession or industry knowledge management requires a holistic and multidisciplinary. Approach to management process and an understanding of the dimensions of knowledge work. It is an evolution of good management process and an understanding of the dimensions of knowledge work. It is an evolution of good management practice sensibly and purposely applied, electronic format which can be access through online and offline both. Electronic resources are becoming popular due to technology changes and advancement now in present scenario we are able to get electronic-resources management across the word within few movements. Electronic resources management are becoming more popular due to its easy access and time saving.

## REFERENCES

[1] Digital Library Federation (2004). Electronic resources management.

[2] Engel, D. and Robbins (2008). Evolving roles for electronic resources librarians. Inyu and Berivold.

[3] How to get started with knowledge Management, extracted from "Exploring opportunities in knowledge management/Boyton.

[4] E-resources management, through portal: A case study of technical information center. *International Conference on Knowledge Management*; 22–25 Feb., 2005, pp. 1–19.

[5] Singh, Pramod Kumar, Knowledge Management Application in Libraries and Information Center DRTC Project-2, 1999–2001.

[6] https://www.researchgate.net

# Digital Services in Academic Libraries: An Innovative Approach

**Kamal Kumar Lal[1], Mamta Chauhan[2] and Asha Negi[3]**

**Abstract**

The article is about innovative university libraries' data services. The aim of the article is to identify possible sources of creativity for library data services and to explain how users will be used to enhance the overall quality of service. Currently, the majority of literature on innovation is extremely focused on library services. Though faculty members have begun to explore university libraries' service innovation process, the industry of service quality remains undeveloped and ignorant. At an even worse time, a crucial study of the multiple service aspects of creative and unique library services has been executed, offering deliberate data on five core innovation alternatives. The document contrasts compare contrasts and incorporate these five creative and progressive alternatives for exploring new university library services and improving the current library Services that might be important to library users. This article additionally makes a study to explore how modern and innovative library services comprise.

*Keywords: Innovative, Disruptive, Service, Technology.*

## INTRODUCTION

> *"Service innovation can be defined as the use and modification of a wide range of emerging technologies. New tech that offers users with enhanced and far more premier library services at an affordable cost is beneficial not only to user modernization but also for society as a whole."*

---

[1] Research Scholar, Himalayiya University Dehradun. Associate Librarian, UPES, Dehradun, India. E-mail: kamal_lal@yahoo.com

[2] Research Scholar, Himalayiya University Dehradun. Assistant Librarian, Govt. (PG) College Maldevta, Dehradun, India. E-mail: mamtac1978@gmail.com

[3] Research Scholar, Himalayiya University Dehradun. Library Assistant, DIT University, Dehradun, India. E-mail: negi6395788819@gmail.com

The Internet initially emerged in the 1950s and even though really do never get widely utilized until the early 1990s. It drastically transformed all aspects of everyday life, such as financial services, amusement, and education. Similarly, it has had a massive effect on library services. Library users also referred to as knowledge hubs, use the Internet to provide their users with fresh collections and assistance. This article will train users about modern library resources and services, their consistency, and their relevance to users. Libraries across the world are facing lockdown issues when it comes to providing access to their own collections and custodian. During the Covid pandemic, various library users developed automated regimes. Libraries with a massive collection of electronic resources may have enough techniques to continue serving users from around the world, even during lockdown times. Remarkable efforts are also being taken to encourage both online and offline access to the library's resources.

## BACKGROUND

Disruptive innovations, such as those suggested by Christensen (1997), have been implemented in libraries and factual offerings, not just library failures, but their appropriateness in the face of certain types of customers and technological change. It is also the failure of a good library or library and factual offerings. The survival of libraries despite technological advances can be attributed to the following hypothetical explanation.

1. Libraries adapt to converting customers' wants and undertake technological advances. In different words, libraries aren't averse to modifications in their environment.
2. The absence of disruptive innovation might cause the failure of libraries and facts offerings. To date, an entire package deal of a progressive library or library offerings has the capacity of changing the libraries in its totality and has now no longer emerged.
3. Looking at how pinnacle-rated establishments failed because of disruptive improvements of smaller establishments, it miles maximum suitable to have a look at whether or not libraries are truly insusceptible to disruptive improvements. This paper is exploratory and descriptive a try to outline progressive offerings inside the mild of disruptive improvements and to examine whether or not a number of that progressive services are disruptive

improvements for the libraries. The paper is likewise primarily based totally on the idea that the theoretical framework of disruptive innovation is relevant to library offerings.

## SCOPE FOR THE LIBRARIES

In order to meet customers' information needs during the pandemic crisis, today's libraries provide a wide range of cutting-edge services. Libraries are the storehouses of knowledge recorded in physical/digital mediums. Modern libraries, in contrast to traditional ones, offer remote access capabilities for their patrons as well as a digital or virtual form of the library collection. E-books, e-resources, digital libraries, e-services, etc. are among the library resources currently in vogue. In addition to recording, storing, retrieving, and disseminating information on a large scale in the form of electronic data, smart libraries' future prospects will incorporate the use of talent and expertise.

## TECHNOLOGY IS CHANGING THE ROLE OF ACADEMIC LIBRARIES

This increasing focus on access to digital resources will undoubtedly affect the role of library professionals. Librarians will be challenged to "learn new skills to be able to apply new technologies to learning, research, and information for their patrons". Earlier readers used to come to the library to read physical books, now readers use e-books and use the internet. In a personal survey, it has been found that readers use digital resources (61.2%), and physical libraries (47.8%) to meet their information needs.

Therefore, it is necessary that the librarian should keep updating his knowledge along with the new technology.

## INNOVATIVE SERVICES OF LIBRARY

- **Use of Web 2.0:** Such innovations will change the face of the library system and revolutionize it. As you all know Demand for smart phones and Android phones is increasing in physical services every day Due to the preference of many library users, what traditional libraries offer is diminishing Library 2.0 service. In addition, continuous evaluation and updates of Library 2.0 Services can meet the changing needs and demands of users Innovative services have no geographical boundaries and anyone from other countries can do it You can use these services without restrictions, just as you would with traditional library services.

- **Big Data:** Simply having more knowledge about the user's thoughts can help the library industry as a whole. Ginny Mies makes the following statement in an article about the use of big data in libraries that were posted on publiclibrariesonline.org: "Libraries can use basic customer intelligence to better reach customers, create better connections with the community, and become more relevant, flexible, and adaptable to any changes in the environment. By delivering material and resources depending on user preferences, libraries can also use big data to tailor user experiences.
- **Artificial Intelligence:** Artificial intelligence is no longer a technology of the future with Siri and Alexa readily available on all platforms today and gaining more and more attention in our daily lives. As many AI apps are geared at giving users information, as Kristin White hair notes in an article on the website Public Libraries Online, this presents a difficulty for libraries. They also add that "intelligence is artificial, not human," though. Unlike AI, libraries can link users to information and—more importantly—to other users. The ability to comprehend user behavior patterns and modify programs to meet their demands is made possible by the addition of a smart side to all of the library's apps.
- **Block Chain Technology:** In the past year, as Bitcoin has gained popularity, blockchain technology has become one of the most talked-about technologies. By storing records of all digital transactions in a decentralized database that is accessible to everyone on the network, blockchain technology provides a promising alternative to centralized databases. It is thus a novel method of gathering and storing data. Sue Alman, a teacher of emerging technologies, noted in an article for Edsurge that block chain technology "Can be used to create an improved metadata system for libraries, to track rights and ownership in a digital-first sale, to connect library and university networks, or even to support community skill-sharing and borrowing programs.
- **Internet of Things:** As Internet connectivity has become more of a necessity than a luxury, The Internet of Things (IoT) is receiving more and more attention. Just like RFID (Radio Frequency Identification), IoT refers to everyday connectivity devices and transfers data between them. But only in the case of IoT, the data is

transferred over the Internet. As a recent article in the American Library Association the site's highlights, there are many "Opportunities for gallery applications, from tracking use the room and participate in the humidity monitoring program for special collections and more". Thus, libraries can provide a better user experience by enriching service and collection.

- **Library Bookmark Apps:** On the "e-book-friendly" website, Piotr Kowalczyk gives several examples of technologies that could be used in the future. The author mentions an interesting device from a Chinese design company Tout, which acts as a regular bookmark but also has additional features to support user activities related to book searches. This tool is still in the design stage but offers the ability to provide directions to the user regarding the book he wants to find or to track his lending activity in a more interactive way. Locating books inside a library is still difficult for many users. A feature that can guide the user to the book is a modern solution to this problem.
- **Digital Interfaces for Printed Books:** The alliance between physical and digital is a development we all look forward to, especially when talking about physical objects. Everyone loves the "copy" and "search" functions of e-books and the highlighting of all the important excerpts from documents. Finger Link is a prototype developed by Fujitsu that provides all digital functions in a printed book. It detects the user's finger and what they are touching and creates an interactive touch screen where they can select the part they want and convert it into a digital form where it can be processed.
- **Quick Response (QR) Codes—Innovative Technology:** Quick Response codes or QR codes are 2-dimensional barcodes that may be scanned by mobile with embedded cameras. Within the automatic identification fields QR code has been wide. These codes may be accustomed to offer quick access to a uniform resource locator, Associate in Nursing SMS message, a sign, a V-card, or any text and QR codes will hold way more info than a daily barcode. The data is encoded in very QR code pictures. This paper targeted QR innovative Technology that uses in fashionable libraries.

  Quick Response code could be a matrix barcode clear by smart phones and mobile phones with cameras. They're generally named second codes, second barcodes, or mobile codes. On most phones purchased within this, one should transfer a free app (application) in order to browse the QR code, though some phones have one preinstalled. Currently, QR Codes uses in many ways like Books, publicity and Identity Cards which are the latest technology.

- **Mobile Technology:** A library is a place where services are offered by librarians to help patrons who require information. In order to save library patrons' time and uphold the fourth law of library science, librarians have implemented a number of ICT-based library services. The following library services can be offered using mobile technology as part of this effort:
  1. Alerts or notifications
  2. Learning Services
  3. Internet Services
  4. Use of online resources
  5. Library Handbook
  6. Document Supply
  7. Consultation Services

## IMPACT OF DIGITIZATION ON LIBRARIES

Digitization has a broad meaning for libraries, including repro-micrographic techniques, technical communication techniques, and additional techniques such as database creation and use. Digitization technology has affected the operations of various areas in the library sections which are given below:

(a) ***Library Management:*** Under this, classification, cataloging, indexing, database creation, CAS and SDI works are affected by digitalization.

(b) ***Library Automation:*** Under this, organizing database, automating the library, and various housekeeping operations are coming which are affected by digitalization.

(c) ***Library Networking:*** Under this, resource sharing and information dissemination are coming which have been affected by Automation.

The following are the four innovation decisions:

1. **Use OPAC and Web OPAC to Search Library Materials:** OPAC stands for Online Public Access Directory. This is a database of a library or library group that allows any library user to access this database for research materials (books, CDs, DVDs, cassettes, videotapes), articles, etc.) are available in the relevant library(s). OPAC can also be used by home library users using Web OPAC.

Such an innovative service saves users time when searching for their essential study materials stored in different libraries.

2. **Library Operation with an RFID System:** Radio Frequency Identification (RFID) is a wireless system that uses electromagnetic fields. This system automatically recognizes and tracks the chip attached to books and library materials. This is one of the self-service programs where library users can get books on their request and automatically list books, usernames, and book release dates are recorded in the electronic register of the library. Institute libraries using an RFID system do not allow users to pick up books or documents unless they have coupons Procedures for registering the books to be delivered and by the users of the books will be followed, which ultimately avoids the risk of theft. To benefit from such library facilities, the user must be a member and the nominal fee for the use of library materials is automatically deducted from the user's bank balance. It also helps to streamline all library materials. Such a system also requires less manpower and helps to reduce the monotonous work of librarians.
3. **NPTEL (National Program for Advanced Technology Learning)**: Electronic means of learning via online web and video courses can be derived from this program. Today, e-learning through online and video courses is changing the face of education and bridging the gap between expert faculties and scholars interested in related subjects. The adoption of NPTEL by libraries can enhance students' understanding and learning. Even students in backward rural areas can use these facilities at a reasonable cost. Classes from CA and CS in Kolkata, Engineering and Medical Entry Preparation in Kota and Management courses in Delhi are specific examples which students benefit from. Even an interested student who has the right internet facilities with optimal speed can make use of these facilities even at home by paying a small fee to the nearby library or paying for the library. Hospitals if away from home through online banking or mobile banking. Experienced faculties of higher technical institutes like IIT, IIM, etc. will also have the opportunity to share their thoughts, beliefs and knowledge with a large number of students without any geographical boundaries.
4. **Inter Library Loan System provided by DELNET**: DELNET was started in January 1988 at India International Center Library and registered as a society in 1992. It was originally supported by the

National Information System for Science and Technology (NISSAT), Department of Scientific Research and Industrial, Government of India. It was later supported by the National Informatics Center, Department of Information Technology, Ministry of Communications and Information Technology, Government of India and the Ministry of Culture, Government of India. http://www.delnet.nic.in.

It is not possible for any library to collect all types of materials and stored these under one roof. The major purpose of such an establishment is to promote the sharing of resources among libraries. A user of a library can use the study materials of another library with the use of DELNET. In this Inter Library Loan System, one library at the request of a library user can bring resources from another library for a specified duration only. Such facilities are quite helpful specifically for research scholars.

## CONCLUSION

The functioning of the library has changed due to the emerging technology in the library. Currently, the information is available in digital format. It is essential for the library staff to keep themselves updated with the current scenario. In this digital age, the responsibility of the library staff increases, they have to educate the library user community according to the new technology. Today's library function not only provides books to the users, but it is also responsible for meeting the information needs of the users in a short span of time. Presently computer technology is replacing the traditional work of the library. In today's digital age, it is accepted that the profession of computer science and library staff will work together to meet the information needs of the information seeker.

Most of the libraries in India are still struggling with the integration of technology to keep up. In India, many organizations like INFLIBNET and DELNET are helping to update academic libraries as per the present digital scenario. The use of technology in libraries has provided many facilities to the users of libraries. Along with saving the time of the readers, the library is always open 24 × 7 × 365. Users can get information as per their timing. Internet connectivity is the basis of the digital library. Therefore, the internet must be available to access the digital library.

## REFERENCES

[1] Alam, I. and Perry, C. (2002). "A customer-oriented new service development process", *Journal of Services Marketing*, Vol. 16, No. 6, pp. 515–534.

[2] Blyberg, J. (2008, January 17). Library 2.0 debased. Message posted to http://www.blyberg.net

[3] Booth, C. (2008). Developing Skype-based reference services. Internet Reference Services Quarterly, 13(2/3), 147–165. Retrieved December 1, 2008, from Library, *Information Science & Technology Abstracts database.*

[4] Booth, C. and Guder, C. (2009). If you build it, will they care? Tracking student receptivity to emerging library technologies in D. Mille R, Ed., Pushing the edge: Explore, extend, and engage. *Proceeding, ACRL 14th National Conference. Chicago: American Library Association.*

[5] Burgle man, J.C., Osimo, D., Pascu, C., Turlea, G. and Ulbrich, M. (2007). The potential disruptive impact of Internet 2-based technologies. First Monday 12(3). Retrieved August 10, 2008, from http://www.firstmonday.org/issues/issue12_3/pascu

[6] Caruso, J., Katz, R., Salaway, G., Kvavik, R. and Nelson, M. (2006). The ECAR study of undergraduate students and information technology. Retrieved July 3, 2008, from http://connect.educause.edu/ecar

[7] Caruso, J. and Salaway, G. (2007). The ECAR study of undergraduate students and information technology: Key findings. Retrieved July 3, 2008, from http://connect.educause.edu/ecar

[8] Chapman, S., Creech, M., Hollar, S. and Varnum, K. (2007). Main library gateway library web survey: Results and preliminary analysis. Unpublished study. Retrieved July 15, 2008, from http://www.Lib.umich.edu/usability/projects/LibGateway.html

[9] Council for Library and Information Resources. (2005). Library as place: Rethinking roles, rethinking space. Retrieved January 22, 2009, from http://www.clir.org

[10] Deiss, K. and Petrowski, M. (2009). ACRL 2009 strategic thinking guide for academic librarians in the new economy. Retrieved March 25, 2009, from http://www.ala.org/ala/groups/divs/acrl/issues/future/acrlguide09.pdf

[11] De Rosa, C., Cantrell, J., Hawk, J and Wilson, A. (2006). College students perceptions of libraries and information resources: A report to the OCLC membership. Accessed June 20, 2008, from http://www.oclc.org/reports/perceptionscollege.html

[12] https://princh.com/blog-8-technologies-to-implement-at-the-library-of-the future/#.YlFp0KpBy M8.

[13] https://knightfoundation.org/articles/five-lessons-for-libraries-looking-toin novate-in-the21st-century

[14] http://www.libsuccess.org/index.php?title=QR_Codes

# Intellectual Property Rights and Digital Rights Management in the Digital Era

**Sanjay Kumar***

**Abstract**

This paper explains the role in managing Intellectual Property right in the Digital Environment library management system and Intellectual property refers to the ownership of intangible goods. This includes ideas, designs, symbols, writings and creations. It also refers to digital media such as audio and video clips that can be downloaded online. Since intellectual property is intangible, if it is stolen, it may be difficult to recover. Say, for example, a person comes up with a great idea for a new invention. Copyright originated in an age where the expression of the intellectual product in physical forms, such as a book. Today, in the information age where digital information can be easily copied at a minimal cost this natural physical limitation to unauthorized copying is removed. It is, therefore, time to reconsider the principle of the copyright model. The purpose of copyright law is to balance the rights of copyright holders and users. Existing copyright law is applicable in the digital age also. As more and more information becomes available in digital format, libraries must ensure that the public can enjoy the same access rights as with printed information. This paper deals with scope and coverage of various concepts connected with IPR, such as intellectual product, patents, copyright, designs, trademarks, computer software, databases, and Internet and cyber laws. Copyright issues associated with digital/electronic information and the protection of the digital right.

*Keywords: Intellectual Property Right, Digital Environment, Cyber Security, Software Library Management.*

* Research Scholar, Kurukshetra University, Kurukshetra, India.
E-mail: sanjayksagwallibgmail.com

## INTRODUCTION

It's a whole new world out there. Intellectual property right, personal information and intangible assets are increasingly at risk from serious data breaches, theft and fraud as well as fetching data protection laws. Today's innovators require a partner with a set of skills beyond servicing patent; trade mark and legal needs. We guide you securely through the whole innovation process. From idea to developed product, our fall range of integrated services guards your technologies and process to maximise the value of your innovation. Data Intellectual Property right is the recent branch of law and with the growth of ICT in recent days, IPR and library study have gained more importance. Knowing the basics of intellectual property rights before discussing the implication of intellectual property rights on library services is felt necessary.

Society values the creative fruits of the human mind, believing that they enrich the fabric of life for all of its members. Thusthe system of laws has been developed that confers rights on the creators of these fruits. These rights are collectively known as intellectual property rights which is commonly abbreviated to 'IPR' (Edenborough, 1997).

TRIPS define intellectual property rights as, the rights given to persons over the creations of their minds. They usually give the creator an exclusive right over the use of his/her creation for a certain period of time (WTO, 2017). The subject matter of intellectual property is very wide and includes literary and artistic works, films, computer programs, inventions, designs and marks used by traders for their goods or services (Bainbridge, 2015).

Primary understanding of the development of intellectual property rights is very important to have basic knowledge of the evolution of intellectual property at the international level. International conventions on different categories of intellectual property giveuniform international standards.

## ORIGIN AND DEVELOPMENT OF INTELLECTUAL PROPERTY

### Paris Convention

Paris Convention is an International Convention, which provides the common platform for protection of industrial property in various countries of the world. Prior to the existence of any international convention in the field of industrial property, seeking protection for industrial property in various countries was difficult due to the diversity of their laws.

Paris Convention for the protection of Industrial property was convened in Paris in 1883 and was initially signed by 11 states (WIPO, 2017) Convention was revised at Brussels in 1900, at Washington in 1911, at The Hague in 1925, at London in 1934, at Lisbon in 1958 and at Stockholm in 1967 and was amended in 1979 (WIPO, 2017).

The Paris Convention addresses patents, industrial design rights, trade marks, well-known marks, names and unfair competition (Colston, 1999). The Republic of India is a member of the Paris Convention since December 7, 1998. At present total, 177 member countries are part of the Paris Convention.

## Berne Convention

Berne Convention was formulated in the year 1886, for the protection of Literary and Artistic Works. "To protect, in an effective and uniform a manner as possible, the rights of the authors in their literary and artistic works" is the aim of the Convention (WIPO, 2017).

Berne Convention protects literary works, artistic works, dramatic works, musical works and cinematographic works and it also protects derivative works based on other pre-existing works, such as translation, adaptations, and arrangements of music and other alterations of a literary or artistic work. Berne Convention states the duration of the copyright protection as 50 years after the author's death. The Berne Convention was revised several times to cope up with the technological challenges that is, first revision took place in Berlin in 1908, followed by the revision in Romein 1928, in Brussels in 1948, in Stockholm in 1967, and in Paris in 1971 (Ahuja, 2015).

## Madrid Agreement

Madrid Agreement was framed on April 14, 1891, which deals with International Registration of Marks and Protocol related to Madrid Agreement, concluded in 1989. Contracting countries to this Madrid Agreement, secure protection for their marks applicable to goods or services, registered in the country of origin, by filling the said marks at the International Bureau of Intellectual Property. Duration of the protection is valid for 10 years and which can be renewed by paying prescribed fees (Arora, 2016). Currently, a total of 100 members is under the Madrid Agreement covering 116 contracting countries.

## World Intellectual Property Organization (WIPO)

WIPO is the global forum for intellectual property services, policy, information and cooperation, which was established in the year 1967. The mission of the WIPO is to lead the development of a balanced and effective international intellectual property (IP) system that enables innovation and creativity for the benefit of all. WIPO has 191 member states and headquarters is at Geneva, Switzerland. WIPO administers conventions namely, PCT—The International Patent System, Madrid-The International Trademark System, Hague—The International Design System, Lisbon The International system of Appellations of Origins, and Budapest-The International Microorganism Deposit System (WIPO, 2017).

## Patent Co-Operation Treaty

The Patent Co-Operation treaty is an International treaty, which assists applicants in seeking patent protection internationally for their inventions. It also helps patent offices with their patent granting decisions, and facilitates public access to a wealth of technical information relating to those inventions. PCT was framed at Washington on June 19, 1970, and the latest amendment to the PCT regulations was donc on 1 July 2017. There are currently 152 contracting countries (Patent Cooperation Treaty, 2017).

## TRIPS Agreement

TRIPS (Trade-Related Aspects of Intellectual Property Rights) Agreement is a multilateral agreement on intellectual property, which came into force on 1 January 1995, TRIPS. The WTO (World Trade Organization) administers agreement. It is an attempt to narrow the gaps in the way these rights are protected around the world, and to bring them under common international rules (WTO, 2017). The agreement operates on a foundation of two of the existing conventions by embodying the substantive provisions of the Paris and Berne Conventions, as well as adding new provisions (Colston, 1999). The types of intellectual property covered by the TRIPSA agreements are copyright and related rights, trademarks, including service marks, geographical indications, industrial designs, patents, layout-designs of integrated circuits and undisclosed information, including trade secrets. It establishes minimum levels of protection that each government has to give to the intellectual property of fellow WTO members (WTO, 2017).

## TYPES and Categories of Intellectual Property Rights

According to WIPO, Intellectual property is divided into two categories that is Industrial Property and Copyright. Industrial property includes patents for inventions, trademarks, industrial designs and geographical indications. Copyright covers literary works (such as novels, poems and plays), films, music, artistic works (e.g., drawings, paintings, photographs and sculptures) and architectural design. Rights related to copyright include those of performing artists in their performances, producers of phonograms in their performances, producers of phonogram their recordings, and broadcasters in their radio and television programs (WIPO, 2017).

### Patents

Patents are granted in respect of inventions, i.e. technological improvements, great and small, which contain at least some scintilla of inventiveness over what is previously known (Cornish, *et al.,* 2010).

As per WIPO, A Patent is an exclusive right granted for an invention, which is a product or a process that provides, in general, a new way of doing something, or offers a new technical solution to a problem. According to Halsbury's Laws of England, the word patent is used denoting a monopoly right in respect of an invention. The patent is a monopoly right conferred by the Patent Office on an inventor to exploit his invention subject to the provisions of Patents Act for a limited period of time (Ahuja, 2015).

Patents are territorial rights and the exclusive rights are only applicable in the country or region in which a patent has been filed and granted, inaccordance with the law of that country or region (Patents-WIPO, 2017).

### Trademarks

According to WIPO, a trademark is a sign capable of distinguishing the goods or services of one enterprise from those of other enterprises. A product can be copied by a competitor and can become outdated by the introduction of new products, but a trademark is unique. A successful trademark is timeless and the most important source of market power and enables its owner to diversify in products and geographical markets (Bansal, 2014).

Internationally trademark is observed under the Madrid protocol. Duration of International registration of a trademark is valid for ten years and it can be renewed for ten years from the expiry of the preceding period. Protection of trademarks in India is governed by The Trademarks Acts, 1999, which is amended in the year 2010 i.e., Trade marks (Amendment) Act, 2010. Registration in India is also valid for ten years and can be renewed time to time in accordance with the provisions of the Act.

## Industrial Designs

According to WIPO, an industrial design may consist of three-dimensional features, such as the shape of an article, or two-dimensional features, such as patterns, lines or colour. In a legal sense, an industrial design constitutes the ornamental or aesthetic aspect of an article. In India, industrial designs are governed under the Designs Act, 2000. "Design" means only the features of shape, configuration, pattern, ornament or composition of lines or colour applied to any article whether in two dimensional or three dimensional or in both forms, by any industrial process or means, whether manual, mechanical or chemical, separate or combined, which in the finished article appeal to and are judged solely by the eye; but does not include any mode or principle of construction or anything which is in substance a mere mechanical device (The Designs Act of 2000).

## Geographical Indications

Geographical indication" in relation to goods, means an indication which identifies such goods as agricultural goods, natural goods or manufactured goods as originating, or manufactured in the territory of a country, or a region or locality in that territory, where a given quality, reputation or other characteristic of such goods is essentially attributable to its geographical origin and in case where such goods are manufactured goods one of the activities of either the production or of processing or preparation of the goods concerned takes place in such territory, region or locality (The Geographical Indications of Goods (Registration and Protection) Act). WIPO expresses a geographical indication (GI) as a sign used on products that have a specific geographical origin and possess qualities or a reputation that are due to that origin. Geographical indications are typically used for agricultural products, foodstuffs, wine and spirit drinks, handicrafts, and industrial products (Geographical Indications WIPO, 2017).

## Copyright

Copyright was recognized only after the invention of printing in the 15thcentury, which enabled the reproduction of books in large numbers. Before that, creative writers, musicians, artists wrote, composed or made their works for fame and recognition rather than to earn a living and question of copyright never arose because copying was a laborious and expensive process (Narayana, 2013). WIPO defines, Copyright (or author's right) is a legal term used to describe the rights that creators have over their literary and artistic works. Works commonly protected by copyright throughout the world include:

1. Literary works such as novels, poems, plays, reference works, newspaper articles.
2. Computer Programs, databases.
3. Films, musical compositions, and choreography.
4. Artistic works such as paintings, drawings, photographs, and sculpture.
5. Architecture; and advertisements, maps, and technical drawings (WIPO, 2017).

## Copyright Law of India

Copyright is a right given by the law to creators of literary, dramatic, musical and artistic works and producers of cinematograph films and sound recordings. In fact, it is a bundle of rights including, inter alia, rights of reproduction, communication to the public, adaptation and translation of the work (Handbook of Copyright Law). "Copyright" means to do or authorise the doing of any of the following acts in respect of a work, such as literary, dramatic or musical work, not being a computer programme, computer programme, an artistic work, cinematograph film, sound recording (Indian Copyright Act of (1957). Copyright in India is governed by the Copyright Act, 1957, which came into effect from January 1958. Further, the act was revised and amended time to time in the years, 1983, 1984, 1991, 1994, 1999, and 2012.

## IPR and Digital Rights

In the digital age, the issue of privacy is an important subject where unauthorized data sharing, data integration, unethical data utilization and unauthorized public disclosure are the major areas of concern.

The major issues are to be considered as follows:

1. Is digitization to be considered as similar to reproduction, for example using Xerox machine?
2. Is digitization a creative activity such as translation from one language to another?
3. Can transmission of digitized documents through the Internet be considered as commercial distribution or public communication similar to broadcasting?
4. Can we consider the database as a special collected work that should be protected by copyright law?
5. What can be considered as fair use in the Internet environment? What are the concerns of the library community?
6. In the digital context if access restricted by the copyright owner, how could the public exercise fair use with those work?

The above issues are specific to the library. The libraries have allowed their users to read a document, to browse through the whole collection; to search through the library catalogue; to supply Xerox copy for research and education purpose; to procure photocopies of articles from other libraries or clearing centres; to widely distribute the re-produced copies of documents for public awareness and to provide interlibrary loan service. Whether all these activities will continue in the digital age? If digitization is considered as reproduction work, it is quite clear that in digitization the initial work is merely changed into the digital form and the process of changing is accomplished by a machine, without any creativity. If it is considered as a translation from one language to another, the digitization is also a change from natural human language into machine language. However, in digitization, there is no creativity involved and it could be considered as a similar activity to reprography. The copyright protects only creative works. Simply transformation into the digital form of an original document cannot be considered as creative work. The transmission of information on the Internet can be considered similar to broadcasting; hence copyright law cannot be applied.

## Ways for Protection of Digital or Intellectual Property

Digital Rights Management (DRM) technologies (also known as Electronic Rights Management Systems) ensure copyright through identifying and protect in the content, controlling access of the work, protecting the integrity of the work and ensuring payment for the access. DRM technologies prevent illegal users from accessing the content. Access is protected through user ID and password, licensing agreements. Another way to protect digital content is through Technical Protection Measures (TPM). These technologies allow publishing companies in securing and protecting content such as music, text and video from unauthorized use. If an author wishes to collect a fee for use of his or her work, then DRM technology can be used. TPM and DRM technologies are increasingly employed to sell and distribute content over the Internet.

### Cryptography

Cryptography is the oldest mechanism employed to ensure security and privacy of information over networks. This involves scrambling (or encryption) of the information to render it unreadable or not understandable language, which only the legitimate user can unscramble (or decrypt). However, cryptography protects the work during transmission or distribution only. After the work is decrypted, it does not provide any protection.

### Digital Watermark Technology

A digital watermark is a digital signal or pattern inserted into a digital document. It is similar to the electronic on-screen logo used by TV channels. A unique identifier is used to identify the work. The message might contain information regarding ownership, sender, recipient etc or information about copyright permission. The system consists of a watermark generator, embedded and a watermark detector decoder. The legal user can remove these watermarks with a predetermined algorithm. The watermarking technology is extensively used in protecting multimedia works.

### Digital Signature Technology

The digital signature includes an identity of the sender and/or receiver date, time, any unique code etc. This information can be added to digital products. This digitally marks and binds a software product for transferring to a specified customer. Digitally signed fingerprints guarantee document authenticity and prevent illegal copying.

### Electronic Marking

In this technique, the system automatically generates a unique mark that is tagged to each of the document copies. This technique is used to protect copyright as well as in electronic publishing where documents are printed, copied or faxed.

### Security Features of Operating System

For the protection of files, data etc. the operating system of a computer such as Windows 2000 Professional, Windows 2000 Server, MS-SQL Server has some unique special security and integrity features.

## CONCLUSION

The socio-economic development of a country depends largely on the creativity of her people and creative works cannot be encouraged without effective administration of copyright laws. Librarians as the custodians of most of the intellectual property cannot be left out in the successful implementation of copyright laws. Violation of copyright laws can easily be carried out in the library. In order to have books, author and creators of literary and artistic works, there should be adequate reward commensurate with the work. Hence, to encourage creativity the enactment of copyright law is essential. Librarian community needs to carry out the war against the violation of copyright laws. The librarians in the digital environment have some responsibility to collect information and help the readers by giving it even if it is an electronic form. Copyright protection should be encouraging creativity and not for creating hurdles in the use of information. The Librarians should work as a catalyst for the free flow of information between the owners of copyright and the users of the information.

## REFERENCES

[1] International Conference on Intellectual Property Rights: Digital Transformation (2019), 2019.

[2] Bhatt, C.V. (2014). Is Digital Rights Management an IPR? *DESIDOC Journal of Library & Information Technology,* 28(5), 39–42. https://doi.org/10.14429/djlit.28.5.214

[3] Bhattacharya, S. and Saha, C. (2011). Intellectual property rights: An overview and implications in pharmaceutical industry. *Journal of Advanced Pharmaceutical Technology & Research*, 2(2), 88. https://doi.org/10.4103/2231-4040.82952

[4] Chattopadhyay, S. (2013). Intellectual Property Rights in Digital Environment. *National Conference on Reprographic Rights and Copyright Act: Challenges and Management*, 146–153. Retrieved from http://eprints.rclis.org/32511/1/Intellectual Property Rights in Digital Environment _ISI.pdf%0A

[5] Handa, S. and Bhatt, K. (2015). Intellectual Property Rights (PR) in Digital Environment: an Overview in Indian Digital Environment. *International Journal of Digital Library Services*, 5(2), 117–123. Retrieved from http://www.ijodls.in/uploads/3/6/0/3/3603729/vol-5_issue-2.117-123.pdf

[6] Hano, T., Ito, M., Ito, K., Kono, K. and Ohkubo, N. (2017). Dietary taurine supplementation ameliorates the lethal effect of phenanthrene but not the bioaccumulation in a marine teleost, red sea bream, Pagrus major. *Ecotoxicology and Environmental Safety*, 137, 272–280. https://doi.org/10.1016/j.ecoenv.2016.12.005

[7] Jadhav, V.G. (2014). Intellectual Property Rights with special reference to Copyright Laws in India. *International Journal of Science and Research (IJSR)*, 3(7), 1130–1133. Retrieved from http://www.ijsr.net/archive/v3i7/MDIwMTQxMjk3.pdf

[8] Kumar, V. and Singh, A. (2015). Impact of Information Explosion on Library Professionals in Digital Technology Scenario. ... of IPR: Challenges for New Age .... Retrieved from http://nlutest.admissionhelp.com/download/publication/2015/Transforming Dimension of IPR—Challenges for New Age Libraries.pdf#page=541

[9] Mir, F.M. (2016). Intellectual Property Rights Issues and Challenges of Academic Libraries in Digital Environment. *International Journal of Computer Engineering in Research Trends*, 3(12), 639–644. https://doi.org/10.22362/ijcert/2016/v3/i12/xxxx

[10] Patel, P. (n.d.). Intellectual, 1–52.

[11] Pathak, P.J. and Das, S. (2001). Utilization of electronic information at IPR Library: a case study. *Information Studies*, 7(2), 109–120. Retrieved from http://search.proquest.com/docview/57491579?accountid=14167%5Cnhttp://www.yidu.edu.cn/educhina/educhina.do?artifact=&svalue=Information+Studies&stype=2&s=on%5Cnhttp://pqdt.calis.edu.cn/SearchResults.aspx?pm=0&q=%5Cnhttp://159.226.100.141/Reader/union_resu

[12] Rights, I.P. (n.d.). CHAPTER III Intellectual Property Rights.

[13] Sinha, M.K. (2015). Role of LIS Professionals in Introducing IPR, Copyrights and Digital Rights Management to University Community in Changing Environment, 2011 (November).

[14] Timings, L., Selection, D., Document, F.A., Grant, B. and Guidelines, G. (n.d.). Guide to Finding a Document.

[15] WIPO (2016). What is Intellectual Property? WIPO Publication, 450(E), 25. https://doi.org/10.1016/j.neuroimage.2005.10.001

[16] Yaranal, M.M. and Ramesha, D. (2012). Managing Intellectual Property Rights (IPR) in Libraries: A Practical Approaches and Solutions. *International Journal of Digital Library Services,* 2(3), 43–50. Retrieved from http://www.ijodls.in/uploads/3/6/0/3/3603729/43-50232.pdf

# Implementation of I.C.T. Towards the Transformation in Library and Information Science (LIS)

**Shalini Tygi[1], Rajni Atrey[2] and Sudhir Tyagi[3]**

**Abstract**

This research paper examines the implementation of information and communication technology (ICT) in library and information science (LIS) education and its impact on the transformation of traditional teaching and learning practices. The study presents an analysis of the various ICT tools and applications currently being used in LIS education, including e-learning platforms, online resources, digital libraries, and social media. It also investigates the challenges and opportunities associated with the integration of these technologies into LIS education and highlights the benefits of using ICT for enhancing student engagement, promoting collaborative learning and expanding access to educational resources. The paper concludes with recommendations for future research on the effective integration of ICT into LIS education and its potential for transforming the learning experience for students and educators alike.

*Keywords: Information and Communication Technology, Library and Information Science, WANs.*

## INTRODUCTION

Information communication technology has resulted in the rapid circulation of knowledge and has transformed information-handling activities in research and academic libraries in India. The emergence of modern library advances in ICT has opened up new ways of accumulating, regulating and disseminating scientific and technical information. Research and academic libraries have already changed their

[1] Rrsearch Scholar, Swami Vivekanand Subharti University, Meerut.

[2] Asst. Librarian, Dev Sanskriti Vishwavidyalaya, Haridwar.

[3] Professor, Swami Vivekanand Subharti University, Meerut.

routine tasks by using effective and efficient information communication technologies to intensify and integrate their electronic resources and services. Finally, librarians in research and academic libraries need to update their knowledge and expertise in information and communication technology (ICT) in order to successfully under take their roles of being responsible for validating the library.

I.C.T. is a relatively new notion that has emerged as a result of the need for innovative educational practices in today's highly competitive global economy. Education of users, information literacy, and the training and development of personnel are all areas where I.C.T. is playing an increasingly significant role.

Education and training are being revolutionised by networked technologies like the internet and the World Wide Web, which allow users to access information and connect with others across geographic borders, cultural contexts, and the globe. There is the possibility of collaborating in groups, exchanging knowledge, and sharing high-quality educational materials thanks to these tools. Training and education are the stated goals of e-learning, which include instruction, assistance, and mediation provided by digital tools. The proliferation of remote education and the establishment of sophisticated systems for the delivery of I.C.T. are only a few examples of the positive effects of the internet on education during the last decade.

Both teachers and students face a bewildering selection of communication options when striving to take full advantage of e-learning. Included in the list of possibilities are:

- learning tools;
- On-Demand Video;
- Internet-based laboratories;
- online lectures;
- online conferences;
- televised shows that are broadcast live;
- computer-generated scenarios;
- a digital evaluation; and
- Administration resources available online.

Different institutions and communities of users have their own unique ways of defining and use of phrases like "e-learning," "technology-based learning," and "Web-based learning" Depending on whom you ask, the term "online learning" might have a number of distinct meanings.

According to Fryer (1997), there are three distinct types of online education:

- A desktop tutor.
- Online course and
- In model number three, we have hyper-interactivity.

Kaplan-Leiserson (2021) However, there is disagreement about the correct use of these phrases and the associated typography. Some individuals may think that the first group is the only one for whom Web-based training is appropriate. The second kind, often known as online learning, is e-learning, which "covers an enormous assortment of utilizations and strategies, for example, online learning, PC-based learning, virtual homerooms, and electronic coordinated effort." The Internet, LANs, and WANs are only a few of the many pathways for content distribution (WANs), audio and video tapes, satellite transmission, cable and satellite, and interactive television and computer-based ROMs.

- **Stokes (2020):** Learning using the Internet and related technologies (including but not limited to computers, multimedia, content portals, search engines, electronic libraries, remote learning, and classrooms facilitated by the World Wide Web) is known as e-learning. The rapid change in technology and mediated human interactions are hallmarks of e-learning.
- **UK's Department of Education and Skills (2022):** From "productive utilization of electronic assets and learning helps with the study hall to a custom-tailored opportunity for growth made conceivable by remote or impromptu access," I.C.T. involves "a range of activities." as defined by the Oxford English Dictionary.
- **Waller and Wilson (2021):** An effective learning process, I.C.T. is the combination of electronically provided information with (learning) support and services."

## Scope of I.C.T.

The use of computers and the internet for education is spreading rapidly over the globe. The effectiveness of online education depends critically on the prevalence of computers and Internet access (Kramer, 2000).

Internet and network-centric computers provide a solid groundwork for I.C.T. innovation and expand conventional education.

Models for training incorporate the utilization of PCs and the Web (Eckert *et al.*, 1997; Colette, 2001). For a number of years now, the Internet and other forms of cutting-edge electronic technology have played an increasingly crucial role in the classroom. The use of electronic

Fruitful, powerful, and of a quality tantamount to a portion of the prior instructive learning frameworks, electronic learning frameworks should utilize these innovations, and attention must be taken in the design and construction of these systems.

Which uses thoughtfully constructed methods and methodologies (Colette, 2021).

## The Importance of I.C.T.

All throughout the workplace, things are shifting due to factors like new technologies, a lack of required skills, increased competition, and other factors. To succeed in today's competitive job market, online education is crucial.

- The economy is changing to one that is more dependent on the spread of information.
- Rethinking education's foundations from the ground up
- Large knowledge gaps need rethinking the current educational system.
- There are several difficulties that have arisen as a consequence of globalisation of business.

## Levels of I.C.T.

I.C.T. may be broken down into four distinct levels, beginning with the most fundamental and progressing to the most advanced. This list will go through many kinds:

### A. *Knowledge Databases*

Information based on programming destinations gives filed clarifications and help for programming requests notwithstanding bit-by-bit guidelines for finishing explicit jobs; in any case, these databases are the most fundamental kind of I.C.T and are not often viewed as actual training.

### Online Support

I.C.T. takes many forms, and online support is one that operates much like a database of information. "Online assistance" encompasses a wide variety of mediums, including forums, chat rooms, online bulletin boards, e-mail, and live instant messaging, all of which are far more interactive than knowledge databases and provide more individualised questions and responses in real-time.

### Asynchronous Training

As the term has been commonly used until recently, this is indeed E-Learning. CD-ROM, network, intranet, and Internet-based self-study all fall under this category. It might be self-contained, connecting students directly to resources in the absence of a live teacher, or it could provide students with access to teachers via channels such as message boards, chat rooms, and e-mail.

### Synchronous Training

There is a live teacher on the line to guide you through the training process in synchronous mode. At the appointed time, all participants check-in and engage in real-time conversation with one another and the teacher. Put up your digital hand and have a look at the electronic whiteboard. Sessions might last just a few hours or they could span months or even years. Common methods of providing such instruction include the use of websites, audio/video conferencing, Internet telephony, and even live, two-way broadcasts to students in class.

The advantages and disadvantages of online education have been discussed at length. The first argument is that students are better able to shift into a mode of motivated and reflective cognition because of the digital information's unique structure. Another argument is that I.C.T. gives students greater freedom of action and response than in traditional classrooms, as well as more frequent and immediate feedback on their progress.

### Benefits to the Instructor

- enables educators to create course materials using the wealth of information available on the Internet;
- facilitates more interesting and effective classroom instruction;

- easy for teachers to get to whenever they need it;
- makes it possible for educators to condense crucial lessons for their pupils;
- Notes conversations and stores them for future reference;
- improves teachers' sense of accomplishment thanks to their students' active engagement;
- Savings on lodging and transportation for training sessions.

Asynchronous, self-paced I.C.T. allows for consistent information delivery.

With effective I.C.T. and knowledge-management systems, not only is specialized information disseminated but it is also captured.

Completion and certification verifications, both crucial components of training programmes, may be automated.

I.C.T. and Teaching in Library and Information Science.

The function of university libraries has evolved and is continuing to evolve in response to IT.

One fascinating result is a heightened focus on the strategic processes within the institution. E-learning, remote education and the growth of virtual universities all rely on libraries' support services. Electronic learning, user training, and support may all benefit greatly from the contribution librarians provide to these processes. Opportunities for those working in the library and information sciences are expanding because of the rise of online education. Expanding access to existing ones, strengthening the information hub's position within the company, and fostering professional growth are all examples. Although online education isn't going to fully replace traditional classroom instruction, it's fast becoming an essential supplementary mode of delivery and opening up new educational possibilities for many. Many library and information professionals utilize I.C.T. to assist students in their work, whether they are on campus or taking classes from afar.

With the advent of I.C.T professionals in the information industry from all over the world may join together in online "communities of practise" to share best practices and build their expertise. Information professionals need to master new methods of instruction, strategies for facilitating online discussions, and tools for collaborating with colleagues from across the world.

## I.C.T. in Digital Libraries

Many academics now use e-mail instead of snail mail, and the majority of our academic libraries have gone electronic. Internet-based tools, such as email with attached files, have made it easier to share and receive information. Inflibnet (web.inflibnet.ac.in/index.jsp), a programme offered by Indian universities' libraries, is expanding quickly in various ways. I.C.T may be integrated into the larger framework of a digital library. In an online classroom, for instance, the materials are always evolving. With every kind of data, there is a method in place to put the user's comprehension to the test. As a result, library services have evolved to better support students' academic pursuits. Both the digital library and online education would benefit from a complementary approach. Recent remarks he made at the Info-vision Summit in this city emphasised the need of having technologically advanced classrooms with user-friendly tools to facilitate e-learning. According to (Large, Andrew, 2005).

I.C.T. and digital libraries have struggled with the spread of associated technologies across national boundaries and user demographics, thus it was crucial that they establish Internet delivery methods and open archives, he added. Flow research is zeroing in on bettering UIs and apparatuses for making content, dissecting information, and cooperating with intricacies. which might make I.C.T. simpler in the future according to (Solvberg, Ingeborg T., 2005).

## CONCLUSION

Despite the fact that online education isn't expected to fully replace traditional classroom instruction, it has quickly become a significant supplementary delivery mode and presents exciting new educational opportunities. Possibilities for a large population. Many library and information professionals utilize learning as a technique to assist students in both traditional classroom settings and independent study. Through online forums and discussion groups, information professionals from all over the world may share ideas and build each other's expertise. This calls for a shift in how information professionals think about education and training, how they interact with students, how they interact with one another, and how they interact with technology. I.C.T. is also starting to affect the organizational structure and operation of information services, especially those involved in education.

## REFERENCES


[1] Lobo, Janet and Bhandi, M.K. E-learning Indian scenario &its impact on library and information science professionals. *4th International CALIBER-2006* held at Gulbarga on February 2–4, 2006. Available at dspace.inflibnet.ac.in/bitstream/1944/568/1/26(cal+06).pdf (Accessed on 26.12.2007).

[2] Sahu, Satya Ranjan and SINGHAL, Madhuresh. E-learning: a myth or reality. Workshop on Information Resource Management. DRTC, Banglore, 2002. Available at http://drtc.isibang.ac.in/~saiful/greenstone/collect/Pdf/index/assoc/HASH01d7.dir/doc.pdf. (Accessed on 24.10.2007).

[3] Roes, Hans. Digital libraries and education: trends and opportunities. D-Lib Magazine. 2001. July/August. 7 (7/8). Available at http://www.dlib.org/dlib/july01/roes/07roes.html (Accessed on 03.01.2008).

[4] Parker, M.B. Three pillars of technology-enhanced–learning. Available at http://general.rau.ac.za/infosci/www2002/Full_Papers/Parker%20M/Parker_TechEnhE-learning.pdf (Accessed on 03.10.2007).

[5] Singh, P.P. and SHARMA, Sandhir (Ed.). E-learning: new trends and innovations. New Delhi: Deep & Deep Publications Pvt. Ltd., 2005. p. 67–68.

[6] SHPT School of Library Science. Prospectus 2007-2008. Mumbai: SHPT School of Library Science, 2007. 59 p.

[7] BORK (Alfred). Learning with the World Wide Web. The Internet and higher education. 2(2); 2000; 81–85.

[8] CHAMBERS (Jack A). The learning Revolution: Electronic classrooms. *Interactive learning international*, 8; 1992; 291–295.

[9] HUANG (Wayne). How to complete in a Global education Market effectively: a conceptual framework for designing a meant generation e-education system. *Journal of Global information management,*12(2); 2004, April–June; 84–107.

[10] Kavitha (R), E-Learning: Success factors and implementation. *SIS (Society for information science: 23rd annual conversion and conference.* I (1); 2005, January 27–29; 469-475.

[11] MALONE (Elizabeth). Seize the day: Developing e-learning context Update, 3(9); 2004, September; 36–39.

[12] SOMASUNDARAM (M). Distance Learning to E-Learning transformation from traditional to virtual education. IJTD. 35 (1); 2005, January–March 37–41.

[13] TOWNLEY (Charles). Using Distance Education to Internationalize Library and Information science scholarship. Libri, 53; 2003; 32–93.

[14] WANG (Meri-Yu). The e-learning library: only a Warehouse of learning resource. The electronic library. 22 (3); 2004; 408–415.

[15] http://www.oecd.org/dataoecd/54/52/23274588.PDF

[16] http://www.blonnet.com/2005/09/19/stories/2005091900950300.htm

[17] JEBARAJ (V. Franklin David) and DEIVASIGAMANI 0(M).The Electronic Library: An Indian Scenario. Library Philosophy and Practice, 5(2); 2003.

[18] www.uidaho.edu/mbolin/lppv5n2.htm

# ICT Based Library System: Traditional to Modern Approach

**Nabina Poudel[1] and Pragyananda Saho[2]**

**Abstract**

In today's era of globalization, Information and Communication Technology (ICT) plays an important role in the management of library systems. The emergence of technology has benefitted the library, which was once just a collection of books in one place. Today, the library is not just a repository of books, but it also contains a large collection of digital resources like e-books, e-journals, and other resources that can be accessed from anywhere, anytime. This paper provides an overview of both traditional and modern approaches to library management systems.

In traditional libraries, there is a need for manpower for performing every task, and later, the concept of cataloging arises, which makes it easier. This paper also examines the challenges faced by traditional libraries and how these have been addressed in modern library systems, along with their features and services. Finally, this paper concludes with various ICT tools like Radio Frequency Identification Technologies, Electronic Resources and common technologies like Virtual Reality, Robotics, social media, Artificial Intelligence, and Cloud-based Infrastructure.

*Keywords: ICT, Library System, Traditional Library, Modern Library, ICT Tools.*

## INTRODUCTION

"Information and Communication Technology" (ICT) came into existence in the mid-1980s, and it consists of three main categories

[1] MCA Computer Science, Dev Sanskriti Vishwavidyalaya, Haridwar, Uttarakhand, India. E-mail: p.nabina2002@gmail.com

[2] MCA Computer Science, Dev Sanskriti Vishwavidyalaya, Haridwar, Uttarakhand, India.

of electronic systems: broadcasting, telecommunications, and mediated communications. The term ICT is a combination of three concepts—Information, communication, and Technology. Information refers to knowledge or meaningful data, communication refers to the Exchange of information, and Technology is used for the exchange of information with the help of computers and communication networks[1].

Overall, it can be concluded as "the combination of all kinds of technological tools, like computers, communication networks along with their applications to process, store, and manage the information".[2]

The emergence and availability of new technologies is the main aspect of the evolution of the library management system. J.E. Rowley (1994) established a four generations framework—The first generation focuses on cataloging and circulation, with its independent modules i.e., no integration. The second generation consists of interconnected modules, with fundamental interfaces and a proprietary based database structure. The third generation arrived with a system based on UNIX and DOCS, user-friendly graphical interfaces, and interconnected and portable systems. The fourth generation had fully integrated import and export of records, client-server architecture, and online catalogs-OPACs (Online Public Access Catalogs). These OPACs have high-quality interfaces and flexible configurations that can now be accessed remotely using the internet[3].

Library Systems were using ICT-based services for fulfilling the requirement of diverse information needs [4] and for providing quality services. A well-planned service-based technology will sustain and help the enhancement of the library. Currently, these libraries were providing access to online databases, Statistical databases, and Full-text information sources world widely[5].

By adopting ICT, libraries became more efficient and automated and reduced repetitive tasks improving the quality of services and easier access to information sources. It enables faster communication, saves time and resources, and improves productivity and adaptation to changing needs in this era[6].

## LIBRARY SYSTEM

The main aspect of libraries, whether they are traditional or modern i.e., ICT (information and communication technology) based is to preserve the knowledge and information throughout the generations. Libraries act as central repositories to store a vast amount of data altogether.

Libraries are used for a variety of purposes including collecting information, improving reading skills, and research purposes. It provides a learning atmosphere that helps human mental development[7].

Most Libraries use Dewey Decimal Classification (DDC) for giving shelf location to the books according to relative location and relative index. Melvil Dewey (1876) first developed DDC. This system also provides a subject-based location for new books. It is used by 200,000 libraries globally[8].

The paper will focus on two distinct types of library systems, i.e., traditional and modern.

## Traditional Library System

These Libraries mainly focused on manual work. Data is recorded in huge registers, for checking the information referring to these registers is the only way. At the time of distribution, well- mannered data is entered in the registers that needs manual support for each of the activities. This is a tough job to maintain the records and data of all the books and arranging them on the shelves, assigning tags to each book with individual IDs. After all of the slow procedures, there is a chance of missing the book. With increasing the materials in the library, the complexity for the management also increases[9].

## Concept of Cataloguing

Catalogues are used for maintaining the records of materials in the library. Various forms of catalogues have emerged, from punch cards, magnetic tape form, printed book catalogs, shelf list catalogues, card catalogues, etc.[10]

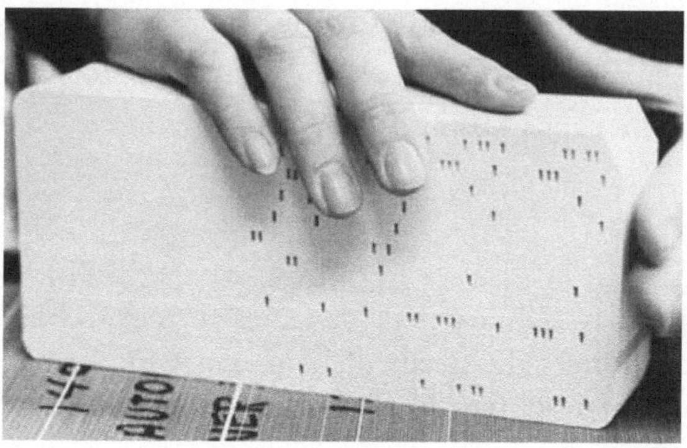

Punch Cards were used for data processing. In this, a particular combination of holes is punched, which represents a particular character. In one card 960 holes can be punched. Magnetic Paper Tape is a punch card reader, which converts it to readable code for the computer.

A card catalogue is a widely used cataloging form of a library catalogue. For card cataloguing, paper cards of fixed dimensions are inserted in the steel rods. These cards were arranged in wooden trays with the required labeling in them.[11]

## Challenges and Limitations of Traditional Libraries

Traditional Libraries are the storehouse of books and other materials. However, these are some challenges and limitations faced:[12]

- Traditional libraries can be accessed only during office hours.
- Finding and locating the information often needs more time spent on it.[13]
- There is a high chance of loss and misplacement of books and resources.
- Increasing resources and users require more staff and storage space.
- Requires manpower for performing all the tasks/operations.
- High maintenance costs for managing resources, staff, and other utilities.

## Modern Library

A modern library is a library that integrates current technology, services, and resources to meet the needs of its users. A modern Library mainly focuses on digital resources like e-books, audio books, databases, and online journals.

In addition to providing access to books and digital resources, contemporary libraries may provide their patrons with an array of services including computer and internet connectivity, educational programs, social events, and community-based activities.

Modern libraries can offer more than just e-books and internet access. They may also provide access to specialized tools and software, such as 3D printers, digital cameras, and software design. Beyond serving as a hub for learning and information, libraries today often function as communal spaces for group meetings, studying, and socializing. Additionally, libraries may partner with other community organizations to provide a diverse range of programs and services.

The incorporation of modern technology into libraries has revolutionized the way they function. Libraries now have access to tools that allow them to enhance their resources, increase availability, and improve the reliability of their services, which would have been difficult to achieve manually. This has transformed libraries from being merely a repository of books into a center for the dissemination of intelligent information. The profound impact of ICT has fundamentally changed the way people perceive and use libraries.

## Services Provided by Modern Library

Libraries are now able to offer an extensive range of innovative services that have become an essential part of any modern library system. Some of these services include providing customized information to users,

- Offering 24/7 access to information,
- Repackaging information to make it more accessible,
- Use selective dissemination of information (SDI) and current awareness services (CAS),
- Having a web-based online public access catalog (OPAC),
- Providing electronic document delivery,
- Implementing automated circulation systems using bar codes or RFID technology,
- Utilizing social networking services,
- Incorporating multimedia and hypermedia, Establishing institutional repositories,
- Offering reprographic services,
- Providing online instruction and reader advisory services,

- Offering online reference services,
- Delivering database services,
- And participating in library networks and consortia[14].

## USE OF ICT TOOLS IN THE LIBRARY

Libraries are leveraging communication technology to enhance their services for users. This includes using ICT tools for functions such as renewing or returning library materials (check-in). Additionally, these tools serve as a means for rapid information dissemination, improving the speed at which information is shared with library patrons.

- **Library Security:** The use of technology has significantly improved library security by implementing various technological processes, including the use of computers. One such technique is RFID (radio frequency identification), which provides advanced security measures for library materials. RFID technology helps to prevent theft and unauthorized removal of library resources, ensuring the safety and security of library collections.
- **RFID Technology:** Modern technology has revolutionized library transactions, particularly around check-in and check-out services. Libraries are now leveraging ICT-based systems to offer fast and user-friendly services. One such technology that has greatly improved library services is Radio Frequency Identification (RFID). By adopting RFID technology, libraries can provide efficient and enhanced services to their users, which aligns with the fourth law of library science - saving the time of the users. This enables libraries to provide quick and effective services, ultimately enhancing the user experience.

- **Resource Sharing:** Information and Communication Technology (ICT) has made it possible for libraries and information centers to share their resources, both in terms of human expertise and materials, with other libraries. Technology has played a crucial role in enabling cooperative acquisition, processing (such as cataloguing and classification), and exchange of information materials, including electronic resources. It has also facilitated joint publication, networking, training of personnel, and staff exchange for seminars and workshops. The significant role of technology in these co-operative efforts cannot be overstated.
- **Electronic Resources:** Modern libraries have expanded their offerings to include electronic resources like e-books, e-journals, and databases, which can be accessed from any location with internet connectivity. These resources provide quick and easy access to a vast range of information for library users.
- **Mobile Applications:** Modern libraries have introduced mobile applications that enable library users to search the catalog, manage their accounts, and access electronic resources using their smartphones or tablets.
- **Data Analytics:** Libraries are utilizing data analytics to gain insights into how their users behave and to enhance their services. This involves studying patterns of resource usage, user demographics, and circulation data.
- **Use of Library Automation Software:** Library automation is a process that involves using technology to streamline library operations and services. It aims to reduce the need for human intervention and increase efficiency while minimizing costs. Library automation software such as Libsys, Koha, and SLIM21 are available for library operations, which automate various library systems such as acquisition, cataloguing, circulation, serials management, and stock verification. ICT is widely used in library housekeeping operations and various library activities and services.
- **Digital Cataloguing:** Librarians have always recognized the importance of cataloguing and classification in making resources available. However, with the help of ICT, even remote libraries can access the vast databases of larger libraries in developed countries to improve their bibliographic data. The availability of online catalogues has drastically changed the way cataloguing and classification is done.

- **Barcode:** Barcode technology has been a part of library automation since the late 1940s, but its first commercial use was not until the 1990s. SB Electronic Systems developed a device called the Telex pen for reading barcode labels. Barcodes are a form of self-contained message that encodes information in a pattern of black bars and white spaces. They represent numbers as a series of 1s and 0s that can be easily read by computers.[15]

9 780201 379624

## TECHNOLOGIES USED IN MODERN LIBRARY SYSTEMS

Modern library systems use a variety of technologies to enhance their operations and services. Some of the common technologies used in modern library systems are:

### Robots

Although not yet widely used in libraries, robots are being tested for various applications. For instance, a growing number of large libraries are utilizing robotic systems to house and retrieve materials. Additionally, robots are employed for tasks such as shelf-reading and managing inventory.[15]

### Virtual Reality

Virtual reality (VR) can transform library instruction by utilizing realistic, immersive scenarios to illustrate how students can use information literacy skills in their daily lives. Traditional information literacy instruction usually involves lectures and technical terms, but VR provides a more engaging and interactive learning experience.

### Social Media

TikTok, a video-sharing social media app, is being used by librarians to create and upload short videos up to 60 seconds in length to promote their library programs, showcase interesting items at the library, share book reviews, and more. These librarians are part of a sub-community on TikTok called Book Tok, which focuses on sharing content related to favorite books using hash tags like #librariansoftiktok and #librarytiktok.[16]

### Cloud-based Infrastructure

Libraries are adopting cloud computing technology to make their services more accessible and flexible. For instance, OCLC has been utilizing cloud computing to share library information through its World Cat service for years. This service is widely used to search for library information and is now available on the cloud, allowing users to access it anytime and from anywhere[17].

### Artificial Intelligence

At the American Library Association's 2022 Annual Conference and Exhibition in Washington, D.C., Soo Young Rieh, professor and associate dean for education at the University of Texas at Austin, acknowledged that librarians have a history of embracing emerging technologies. However, while AI-enabled technologies such as Siri, Alexa, Uber, and Lyft have become part of everyday life, libraries have been slow to adopt AI. Clara M. Chu, director of the Mortenson Center for International Library Programs at the University of Illinois at Urbana-Champaign, emphasized this point[18].

### Launchpad

To address the digital divide and provide access to technology for low-income library users, the Las Vegas-Clark County Library District introduced 1,050 Launchpads in 2022. These tablets contain content from the Pre-K Academy and Reading Academy, as well as Super Packs with double the number of apps. The tablets are fully cataloged and can be checked out from any of the 25 LVCCLD branches, providing access to educational resources and technology for all library users.

## FEATURES OF ICT-ENABLED LIBRARIES

- ICT has brought significant changes in the way libraries operate. The use of ICT in libraries has made it possible to manage resources efficiently, measure usage and evaluate the impact of resources.
- Libraries are now providing information about Open Access resources and building Institutional Repositories.
- They also providing seamless integration to different databases, and electronic and online resources.

## CHALLENGES FACED BY THE ICT ENABLED LIBRARIES

- However, implementing and maintaining ICT devices and software requires a considerable amount of funds.

- ICT advances too frequently and requires regular updating, leading to a continuous expense that can be challenging for libraries that are often scarce of funds.
- As libraries advance in terms of new services, the expectations of users increase, and libraries need to keep up with these expectations to enhance users' satisfaction.
- Libraries need to have tech-savvy staff who can fully exploit and innovate ICT-enabled library services.
- Regular training of library staff is necessary to cope with the frequently upgraded ICT devices and software.

Libraries must update and renovate their services to keep up with their changing roles. Educating users about the use of ICT-based libraries is also essential, which can put an extra load on libraries.

## CONCLUSION

With the continuous evolution of technology, it is important to cope with the current technology and requirements. The adaptation of ICT-based libraries has transformed the traditional library. But both Traditional and Modern libraries have different kinds of services they provide to users. Regarding what to use? Traditional or Modern, Hybrid Libraries will fulfill the diverse needs and preferences of users. Hybrid libraries merge print and digital materials to provide access to diverse information resources, from anywhere. This is made possible by a single, integrated interface for a seamless user experience.

So, adopting a hybrid library with updated ICT-based technology will cater to the changing needs of users in the digital age.

## REFERENCES

[1] Parvez, A. (2011). Development in library services with the advent of ICT based products & services: A continuous process, *International Journal of Digital Library Services*, Vol. 1, Oct.– Dec. 2011, Issue 2.

[2] Azmi, R. and Nishat, F. (2008). Impact of Information and Communication Technology LIS: Major shifts and practices, *6th International CALIBER University of Allahabad*, Allahabad 2008 .

[3] Rowley, J. The electronic library. Brasília, DF: Briquet de Lemos/Livros, 2002. 399 p.

[4] Adebayo, Odunola Adefunke; Ahmed, Yakub Olayinka and Adeniran, R. Toyin, The role of ICT in provision of library services: A panacea for

sustainable development in Nigeria (2018). *Library Philosophy and Practice (e-journal),* 1951.

[5] Hussain, Akhtar, "The ICT based library and Information services: A case study of B-Schools in Delhi and NCR region" (2013). *Library Philosophy and Practice (e-journal).* 1011.

[6] Ramana, P.V., Information Technology Applications in Libraries. New Delhi: Ess Ess Publications, 2004, pp. 24–66.

[7] Shodhganga: A reservoir of Indian theses @ INFLIBNET. (6044, October 10). https://shodhganga.inflibnet.ac.in/bitstream/10603/396044/10/10_chapter01

[8] Dewey Decimal Classification (n.d.). Wikipedia. https://en.wikipedia.org/wiki/Dewey_Decimal_Classification.

[9] Shanmugam, P., Ramalakshmi, A., Ganeshan, S. and Shanmugam, P. (2020). Library Management System. *Research Gate.* DOI: 10.37896/JXAT12.11/29777

[10] Certificate in Library and Information Science (n.d.). https://nios.ac.in.

[11] Chinnasamy, K. and Nachimuthu, R. (2009, March 26). The Information Generation System from Traditional to Modern Library. Research Gate.

[12] Garg, M. (2013). Libraries in the Era of ICT: An Overall Transformation. *International Journal of Library and Information Studies,* ISSN: 2231-4911, Vol. 3(1) Jan.–Mar., 2013.

[13] Traditional Library—Library & Information Science Education Network (2022). *Library & Information Science Education Network.* LISBDNETWORK (2022b, February 14).

[14] Garg, M. (2013, June). Libraries in the Era of ICT: An Overall Transformation. *International Journal of Library and Information Studies,* ISSN: 2231-4911, Vol. 3(1), (Jan.–Mar., 2013).

[15] Smith, C. (2020, May 28). What the Future Holds, American Libraries Magazine. *American Libraries Magazine.*

[16] Panuncial, D. (2022, October 25). 60 Seconds of Library Fame | American Libraries Magazine. *American Libraries Magazine.*

[17] Mondal, H. (2021, July 13). Overviews of Cloud Computing and Its Role in Modern Library Services. Emerging Issues in Commerce, *Economics, Information Technology and Management* (Vol. II) (pp. 218–238).

[18] We Can't Ignore AI | American Libraries Magazine (2022, June 26). *American Libraries Magazine.*

# Electronic Resources in the Information Centers: A Managerial Overview

**Usha[1] and Yanti Raj[2]**

**Abstract**

ICT has a major impact on the material for research. This is changing the size of primary and secondary resources like as text, data, images, such as catalogs and bibliographies. Electronic resources have become the most popular tool for Information centers in the present era. With the demand of technology, Information centers are moving to electronic resources. How to manage electronic resources in Information centers for better information services, the objective of this research paper.

*Keywords: CD-ROM, by Electronic Resource Management, OPAC, Cooperative Library Information Network, Electronic Information Processing System.*

## INTRODUCTION

Information centers have been greatly affected by the changes in information technology, the pace of changes is still fast in this era. Information technology is now capable of generating: (i) new products, processes and machines that can be used independently, adapted information packages cassettes,, video, information products, personal computers and reprographic equipment (ii) external dependent, (iii) Cooperative library information network and (iv) Electronic information processing system such as database online information system.

## ELECTRONIC RESOURCES

Electronic resource is that electronic products that provide a collection of data, whether full text, e-journals, image collections, other multimedia

[1] Library assistant, Dev Sanskrti Vishwa Dev Sanskriti Vishwavidyalaya, India. E-mail: usha.dsvv@gmail.com

[2] Library assistant, Dev Sanskrti Vishwa Dev Sanskriti Vishwavidyalaya, India. E-mail: Yantiraj10111987@gmail.com

products, text based and numerical, graphical or time based, commercially available to published with objective of marketing. These can be delivered on CD-ROM, by tap, through the Internet, etc. According to Barker, there are three types of documents used in selection of electronic resources.

## SELECTION OF ELECTRONIC RESOURCES

Selection is not a new term of library professionals and they have been doing it since long before libraries began to procure printed resources. However, libraries are now focusing on the demands of electronic resource, and moving towards electronic resources instead of printed resources. In fact, especially in the presence of the Internet as a new means of information disseminating, there are a large number of web-based full-text online resources.

The process of holding e-resources should be in accordance with the demands of users, recommendations of users, etc. In addition, the following way should be used in this:

To know the wishes of the library users;

- • The Determining the scope of electronic resources;
- • Checking the quality of that resources search facilities;
- • know the resources according to user demand;
- • The time of receipt; subscription based or web based checking;
- • Technical Support and System.

Licensing agreements evolutions;

- To updated application software and installation;
- Orientation programs and training.

### Assessment of Electronic Resource

Electronic resource becomes more important due to the large number of digital resources available on the internet like databases, e-text, e-journals, etc. Intended audience, authority, currency, use accuracy, etc. are some of the authentic criteria for evaluating digital resources. Due to this, the comprehensiveness of the content, accessibility, quality and technical support, cost, terms of the license agreement is also other responsible factors that may be taken into consideration.

Electronic resources consider aspect as following:

- As mostly electronic resources do not include data prior to some year so identify the electronic version have the data presentation.
- Offer any special features which are not available in other print version; particular source of electronic resources.
- The electronic resources content with significant to the users.
- Updating of versions to make sure.
- reasonable price and compare with other host institutions
- To identify the method of data entry of electronic resources available;
- To identify the electronic resource maintenance and restore the libraries websites.
- To check the library staff training and support with the existing technology.

## Management of Electronic Resources

Management of resources in information centers is one of the important and tough tasks for smooth functioning of excellent services in information centers. As such, the system administrator must have good professional skills in order to completely organize the available resources. In a Information center, the professional must have knowledge such as computing, database management, networking and other ICT skills related to the IT environment. Therefore, while organizing electronic resources, the system Administrator may consider the following:

- Maintain a OPAC or to make another list for browsing.
- Manage and organized under a separate authority with host server.
- Access provide by alphabetical or under separate subject headings.
- To maintain the electronic resources as per the context of other websites.
- To check abstracting or full text access to electronic resources.

Than most of the users search of resources under subject heading and organization of electronic resources may be in such a way that the users may be able to retrieve different search systems form information resources.

## Challenges to Managing Electronic Resources with Present Era

The use and management of electronic resources has many advantages over library services. Users are aware with such services that they can easily get their needed information within a little period of time. Information centers face a variety of tuff time as they try to continue offering the quality of information and services that users have come to expect. Some of the challenges faced by electronic resource management as mention.

- **Preservation:** Electronic information resource is facilitating information to be, disseminated created, manipulated and located with preserving access to this information possess a great challenge. Unless, preservation of electronic information is mostly taken, the information will become vide to get to due to changing ICT platform and media instability.
- **Unskilled Professional:** Due to lack of managing and technical skills, the professionals of library is not able to manage the electronic resources. The library professional staffs are required to continuously update their own skill and knowledge base so as to work in today's vast changing electronic environment.
- **Inadequate Fund for Library:** Most of the information centers have inadequate fund for obtain electronic resources and so the users not able to get their needy information at the right time. Information Centre are at a disadvantage when acting singles in this environment and there is need for industry purchasing through library consortia.
- **Infrastructure of ICT:** Infrastructure such as software, hardware, internet facilities in a electronic information service system, and other physical equipments are required to provide as infrastructure setup of Information centers, comprehensive access to information electronic resources.
- **Cooperation Gap of Library Staff Members:** The support and cooperation of library staff members, programmers and technical staff are very poor to provide effective service in a electronic environment.

## CONCLUSION

In this age of digital era, the world has changed into a global village. The uses of electronic resources with ICT comfort are one of the important aspects of among the various users groups. Users groups demand to use for electronic resources to provide there needed information. Electronic resources totally changed the way of information gathered, organized, accessed and consumed. Electronic resources have brought to bear a great influence on the academic and professional competence of the users community.

## REFERENCES

[1] Bentil, W. (2020). Electronic Resource Management and Usage in Academic Libraries: The Ghanaian Context.

[2] Bothmann, R.L. and Holmberg, M. (2008). Strategic planning for electronic resource management. In Electronic resource management in libraries: Research and practice (pp. 16–28). IGI Global.

[3] Gul, S. and Bano, S. (2019). Smart libraries: an emerging and innovative technological habitat of 21st century. The Electronic Library.

[4] Hiremath, B.K. and Anand, K. (2015). Mobile technology based information services in the digital world. *International Journal of Development Research.*

[5] Kenchakkanavar, A.Y. (2014). Types of e-resources and its utilities in library. *International journal of information sources and services*, 1(2), 97–104.

[6] Laltlanmawii, R. (2011). An Evaluation of Use of E-Resources in Indian Institute of Technology Library, Guwahati.

[7] Sadeh, T. and Ellingsen, M. (2005). Electronic resource management systems: the need and the realization. New Library World, 106(5/6), 208–218.

[8] Yu, H. and Breivold, S. (Eds.). (2008). Electronic Resource Management in Libraries: Research and Practice: Research and Practice. IGI Global.

# Implementation of ICT Towards the Transformation of Library and Information Science

**Magan Singh Bhandari***

**Abstract**

The development of Information Communication Technology and implementation of it`s in Library and information Science has totally changed traditional Library and Information Science services in to computer-based services. The Implementation of ICT in Library and Information Science Services has the objective of introducing the various aspects of ICT so as to enable these aspects in library and information science services. We have to acquire the competence create databases of holding libraries and then digitize the resources. Digitization is a process of converting the content of physical media in to digital format. As all the recorded information in traditional libraries were analogue in nature. However, the analogue information is fed into a computer; it is broken in to 0s and 1s changing its characteristics from analogue to digital. After digitization the library automation software were developed for automation of library. All housekeeping operations e.g., acquisition, cataloging, administration and circulation etc. are performed by library automation software. Now the libraries have come from being mere repositories of books and other published documents, limiting themselves to just circulation of documents. The library and information science center's now have a lot of e-form documents e.g., e-books, e-texts, e-journals, etc. A number of innovative services such as Alternating services, Bibliographic and Literature search services, Reference services, Referral services and Document Delivery services etc. are being offered by modern libraries now. The internet is also playing a vast role in modern libraries with the help of which all online services are performed by library and information centers. Internet have become as one of the most powerful media of

* Research Scholar, OPJS University, Churu, Rajasthan, India.
E-mail: maganbhandari1@gmail.com

communication. The Internet and associated technologies have transformed the world in to a global village defying the limitations of geographical boundaries. Near about two decades ago most of the people knew very little or nothing about internet but now people are not feeling comfortable without internet. The Internet is the world`s largest computer network which enables computers to all kinds of communication and share services. The Internet is like an architecture which provides communication capabilities as well as information services. Internet plays a vast role in implementation of ICT towards the transformation of Library and Information Science.

Implementation of ICT Towards the transformation of Library and Information Science may be stated in following steps:

1. Database Management.
2. Digitization of Library and Information Science Centers.
3. Automation of Library and Information Centers.
4. Library and Information Services.
5. Internet resources and services in Library and Information Science.

## DATABASE MANAGEMENT

Data is known as the raw material from which the information is derived as the final product. Database management system has two important functions viz... Retrieval and maintenance. Retrieval refers to reading data from files to fulfill information requirements of the users while maintenance concerns changing of data and stored files. Database system for management support is referred to Management Information System. So, for implementation of ICT towards the transformation of library and information science the database is managed. The artificial Intelligence is developed in computers. The artificial intelligence is a group of related technologies that attempts to develop machines to emulate human-like qualities such as seeing, learning, hearing, reasoning and communicating. There are three goals of database management system. i. To provide retrieval flexibility. ii. To ensure high level data independence. iii. To elimination of multiple copies of master file and facilitate reduction of data duplication. Thus for the Implementation of ICT towards the transformation of Library and information science database is managed.

## DIGITIZATION OF LIBRARY AND INFORMATION SCIENCE CENTERS

All recorded information in traditional library are in analogue form which include printed books manuscripts, cards, periodic articles, photographs, audiotapes and video texts. When analogue information is fed in computers it is broken in to 0s and 1s changing its characteristics to digital. These bits of data can be compressed in storage. Flexibility is assets of digital information. The word digital` describes any system based on discontinuous data. Digitization is the first towards making a digital library. It is specialized and cost intensive process that requires input from diverse branches of knowledge. The planning of project for digitization is to perform carefully which includes managerial planning, hardware & software planning, human resource planning and financial planning. Digitization enables documents accessible from the website of libraries. Digital cameras and optical scanner are used to digitize images by translating them in to bit maps. The process of digitization includes four steps scanning, indexing, storage and retrieval. The scanned document remains picture of printed page. Now most of the books or documents have been changed in to digital form.

## AUTOMATION OF LIBRARY AND INFORMATION CENTERS

Housekeeping operations e.g. Acquisition, processing, circulation and maintenance are usually performed by Library automation software in modern libraries. Library automation process is started by Librarian—Dr. John Shaw Billing. Herman Hollerith. A Census Bureau of USA employee who invented punched card machinery. Hollerith formed the tabulating machine Company in 1896. This letter became International Business Machine. Now modern form of; Library automation software are developed. A good library automation software package should fulfill the expectation of library users, staff. It should perform library activities and services, user friendly, flexibility for customization of software other relevant aspects. A software should capable of satisfy general system requirements and functional requirements. Some Library Automation Software with their organization are as follows;

Table 1

| *S. No.* | *Library Automation Software* | *Developer Organisation* |
|---|---|---|
| 1. | Acquas | Over information system Kolkata |
| 2. | Archives | Minifax Information System Kolkata |
| 3. | CDS/ISIS | UNESCO |
| 4. | D-Space | – |
| 5. | E-Granthalaya | N.I.C. New Delhi |
| 6. | GOLDEN LIBRA | INSDOC New Delhi |
| 7. | Integrated Library Management Software | Pragati Computers Pvt. Ltd. |
| 8. | KOHA | Katipo communication Ltd. Newzealand |
| 9. | LIBMAN | Detapro consultancy, Pune |
| 10. | LIBRA | I.V.V. System Ltd. New Delhi |
| 11. | LIBRARIAN | Soft-Ed, Pune |
| 12. | Library Management | Detametics Pvt. Ltd. Mumbai |
| 13. | Library Management | Indo Informatics, Bangaluru |
| 14. | Library Management | Reyan systematics, Bangaluru |
| 15. | Library Management | U&I Software Pvt. Ltd., Mumbai |
| 16. | Library Manager | System Data Control Pvt. Ltd., Mumbai |
| 17. | Libsoft | E.T. & T. Corporation New Delhi |
| 18. | Libsys | Libsys Corporation, New Delhi |
| 19. | Listplus | Computer Systems Bangaluru |
| 20. | Loansoft | Computec Computer System |
| 21. | MECSYS | MECON, Ranchi |
| 22. | MAITRAYEE | NISSAT |
| 23. | NIRMALS | Nirmal Institute |
| 24. | NLIS | Asmita Consultant, Mumbai |
| 25. | SALIM | Uptron India Ltd. New Delhi |
| 26. | SLIM-1.1 | Algoritham, Mumbai |
| 27. | SOUL | UGC, New Delhi |
| 28. | Tulips | TATA Unisis Ltd. Mumbai |
| 29. | ULISYS | Wipro Information Ltd. Secundrabad |
| 30. | Vertua | Verginia America |
| 31. | WILSYS | Wipro India, Bangaluru |

## LIBRARY AND INFORMATION SERVICES

Modern libraries are now come to way from being mere repositories of books and other publications. The types of services given by libraries changed: libraries have a lot of e-documents e.g. e-books, e-journals, e-texts, e-magazines, e-thesis, e-annuals etc. A number of innovative services are now offered by libraries on online basis. The implementation of ICT in library and information science services enables many services e.g. Document delivery service, Circulation of books, Alarting service, Bibliographic and Literature search service including full text service, Reference and referral service, current awareness service and Document delivery service etc.

Forms of current awareness service:

1. list of addition.
2. Current content list.
3. Bulletins.
4. Research in progress.
5. Employment information.
6. News filtering service.

Besides these services, study of user's attitude towards library and information services, Study of Information seeking behavior of users in library and information science centers, users training, staff training, seminars, meetings are also organized by library and information centers to improve the qualities of services.

## INTERNET RESOURCES AND SERVICES IN LIBRARY AND INFORMATION SCIENCE

The Internet is the network of networks. The term internet is coined form of interconnection and network. The network is the group of computers that are connected together for sharing information and their resources. Several network joined together across the world is known as internet. The internet is most powerful media of communication. The internet has changed the whole like a global village. The internet has revolutionized the methods of communications world. The internet is integration of many services and functions rolled in to one. It has mechanism for information storage, world-wide broadcasting facility, a media for electronic publishing of scholarly literature, a medium for collaboration. The internet is a example of most successful sustained investment. It is a commitment to research and development in infrastructure of information science. The government, industry and academia became partners in deploying and evolving this exciting new technology of Internet.

Although it is often stated that to control the activity the Internet does not have any central authority. But there are well known organizations that work together and make domestic environment to collectively participate in development, research and management.

Thus Internet plays a vital role in implementation of ICT towards transformation of library and information science. By means of communication internet has become a key word without which communication is not possible in field of Library and Information science technology.

## REFERENCES/BIBLIOGRAPHY


[1] Anderson D. (1989). Standard practices in the preparation of bibliographic record, London IFLA UBCIM.

[2] Gredley. E. and Hapkinson, A. (1990). Exchanging Bibliographic Data: MARC and other international formats. Otawa: Canadian Library Association.

[3] Rowley, J. (1998). The Electronic Library London: Library Association.

[4] Noerr, Peter (2000). Digital Library Tour Kit USA: Sum Microsystem.

[5] http://WWW.sun.com/products-n-solutions/edu/libraries/digitaltoolkit.html

[6] Arms William, Y. (2000). Digital Libraries the MIT Press: Cambridge. MA.

[7] Evolution of Internet Resources in the Librarians' Index to internet (2002). Available online (http://lii.org).

# Libraries in the 21st Century: Redefining Their Future Through ICT

**Sanjiv K. Sain[1] and Asha Negi[2]**

**Abstract**

This Research paper focused mainly on Libraries in the 21st century. How they are using Information and Communication Technology (ICT) to rethink& redefining their future. This research starts by emphasizing the importance of ICT in how & to what extent for Users and scholars use libraries. Libraries make a difference in people's lives. They encourage a positive approach to life in the role models of tomorrow. As a result, it is critical to ensure that they receive a world-class education at twenty-first-century libraries. The paper goes on to discuss the services provided by twenty-first-century libraries, such as Web-based Reference Services, Selective Information Dissemination, Current Awareness Services, and an Online Public Access Catalogue. The aspects of twenty-first-century libraries are highlighted. This will also include multi-user access to resources, improved operations, 24/7 service, and other benefits. This research article evaluates the role of information technology resources in the transformation of library services. It starts off with a comprehensive history of academic libraries before moving on to a discussion of the opportunities and challenges facing academic libraries today. After that, it offers thoughts on how academic libraries are evolving, as seen, for instance, by the decline in physical book stock and the rise in collaborative learning environments. The article also includes examples of cutting-edge technical advancements for data management and learning, as well as how they have affected university libraries, including the necessity for personnel to acquire new skills and take on "embedded" librarian positions. This research paper finishes with thoughts about upcoming innovations and the function of IT tools.

---

[1] [1]Librarian, DIT University, Research Scholar, Himalayiya University, Dehradun, India. E-mail: sanjivsain74@gmail.com

[2] Library Assistant, DIT University, Research Scholar, Himalayiya University, Dehradun, India. E-mail: negi6395788819@gmail.com

***Keywords:*** *21st Century, ICT, Information, Digital, Transformation, Library.*

## INTRODUCTION

Academic literature and the point-of-fact push have examined the idea of technology as a force of "digital transformation" in the library industry. The IT department organized the "Libraries of the Future" working group. An overview of some of the most important technological advancements pertinent to the industry is provided, along with analysis and reflection on the important subjects that were discussed and debated within the group. While identifying the role of IT services within a broader framework and the historical development of the academic library service, this research article also explores how these developments have affected the professional duties and practices of academic library professionals. This research examines the difficulties that library users have across all categories. Libraries are essential for the preservation of libraries' print and digital resources as well as the dissemination of information to users. Libraries must recognize the current trend toward digital formats for library materials because users seek to connect libraries and their resources both physically and virtually.

Libraries must diversify and embrace new technologies in order to become more than just book repositories. A library serves as a resource center and activity hub for learners. Traditional to digital library transformation is a global trend that necessitates collaboration between government and non-government organizations. To encourage more digital initiatives, basic connectivity and data management infrastructure must be in place. Libraries have been greatly influenced by information technology, with the majority of strategic and tactical activities and procedures relying on IT devices such as the internet, Wi-Fi connections, and so on.

In order to maintain library functions as important values for preserving information heritage and technological knowledge, library management must take on new roles and responsibilities. To overcome transformation, libraries and librarians must be aware of the challenges and opportunities, acknowledge the impact of the change, and ride with the transformation in order to stay ahead of others and remain at the forefront of it.

## OBJECTIVES OF THE LIS SECTOR

The following objectives are what LIS professionals work to achieve in their various information roles in various types of libraries:

1. Promote and assist all communities across the nation in their economical, educational, cultural, recreational, scientific, technical, and informational growth.
2. Make sure that everyone gets the most efficient access possible to pertinent information.
3. Promote information literacy, a reading culture, and basic and functional literacy.
4. Supporting independent and critical thought as well as intellectual freedom will strengthen democracy.
5. By employing new information and communication technology, library and information services can be provided in a more streamlined, equitable, efficient, and high-quality manner (ICT).
6. Provide everyone, especially those with impairments, access to the nation's documentary history and to global information resources.
7. Provide services for conservation while ensuring the preservation of the nation's documentary history.
8. By gathering and distributing it in book, audio, and video media, we can mainstream and value indigenous knowledge.

## LIBRARIES GROWING ORGANISM

A significant part of academic research, instruction, and scholarly communication, libraries have a long history and rich tradition. From huge, internationally recognized collections to dispersed, federal campuses, there are many diverse library models. After World War II, scholarly production significantly increased, and the advent of early computing technology resulted in the creation of new systems for the organization, cataloging, and retrieval of data. Nonetheless, there have been worries that automation and digital services could cause libraries to disappear and eliminate the need for librarians. Libraries had to shift to electronic services in order to provide "value-added" services.

The emergence of new roles and methods of service delivery, such as seamless information architecture and knowledge organization structures, have been made possible by digital innovations for library workers. Libraries have been rearranged as a result of blended learning; recent examples include the University of Worcester's Hive, Sir Duncan

Rice Library, and Philological Library. Yet, due to budget cuts and pressure on service delivery, many library services in higher education have suffered, which has led to increased responsibility for managing research data and open access obligations as well as efficiency savings. These difficulties and possibilities will be more thoroughly examined in this research article.

## The Library's Function in Managing Research Data and Open Access

Academics, publishers, and research communication have all been greatly impacted by the movement toward open-access publications. Libraries should pay particular attention to research data management. Current Research Information Systems (CRIS) provides support for institutional research information management, and agencies like the Digital Curation Centre provide resources and cross-institutional assistance. Others, though, ponder if libraries have the capacity and know-how to undertake these new responsibilities.

## Library IT Services for a Dynamic Educational Environment

Libraries must be able to support diverse and international university learning communities, comprehend and be responsive to all international students' needs, and invest in skill development and ongoing improvements in order to provide effective, meaningful, interactive, flexible, and culturally aware library services and programs. Web 2.0 tools like RSS feeds, social networking sites, audio and video podcasts, and blogging are used to inform users about the library. Additionally, these tools enable the development of a participation framework for increased knowledge sharing, collaboration, and invention. Online reading lists are increasingly frequently used to create, change, personalize, update, and incorporate reading lists into online learning and teaching materials. As there are several ways that eBooks are made available, different expectations of libraries, faculties, and eBook suppliers, as well as a lack of uniformity and restrictive circumstances, academic libraries struggle with the choosing, licensing, procurement, management, and promotion of eBooks. A substantial amount of influence may be exerted on the environment for e-books by library staff.

## Mobile Devices and Social Media

As new technologies, such as mobile technology and "smart" gadgets, become more prevalent, academic libraries are under growing pressure to keep up. Children are more likely to prefer reading on a computer screen over a physical book or magazine, according to a survey of 8 to 16-year-olds.The most active users of social media are libraries, which encourage participation, embrace openness, and reach a larger audience. Social media technologies can be used to establish a powerful online presence and a contemporary image, develop services online, share service and product updates on social media tools, and offer affordable options for promotional and marketing collateral. With the use of interactive reference services, video tutorials for database use, and Lib Answers, libraries may also use social media to train their patrons in information literacy.

## Gamification and Blended Learning

People gather in maker spaces to create things, and 3D printers are seen as chances to democratize cutting-edge technology. Gamification, which improves user engagement and learning, is the usage of game design concepts in contexts other than games. The possible negative effects and repercussions of poorly planned gamification projects are a source of concern, though.

## The Significance of Digital Literacy in Libraries

In spite of the fact that librarians place a high value on digital literacy, students frequently fall back on outdated search and browsing techniques. Instead, students used a consistent and predictable research technique, starting with course readings and Google, according to a poll of 2,318 respondents. This suggests that it is essential to critically assess innovative approaches to providing information services on a broad scale, as well as their consequences for academic librarians and their own activities.

The duties of library employees have changed to stress keeping up with cutting-edge digital trends, developing technology, and modern approaches to information access, usage, sharing, and communication. Other transferrable abilities, such as teaching and training with references to new media and learning methods, are becoming more and more in demand. For library employment, candidates must possess both traditional librarianship skills and technological and instructional design expertise. It might be challenging for librarians to implement and teach pre-established educational and instructional paradigms.

## Educating and Empowering Academic Librarians

The integrated or blended academic librarianship approach focuses on creating a relationship between academics and librarians in order to put librarians at the Centre of the learning process and make them active participants in the processes of teaching, learning, and assessment. Embedded librarians provide a wide range of additional services in addition to teaching, research, current awareness and alerting services, reviewing the literature, and managing web content. It gives academic libraries new responsibilities, such as promoting students' information literacy growth and upholding more collaborative academic methods. The use of social media platforms by researchers is encouraged and supported, which promotes and supports research. In order to better engage with academic staff, libraries must stay up to date on new results.

## The Status of the Library Profession

Libraries' social role is being hampered by the profession's low standing and practitioners' uncertainties about their own professional identities. As a result, there has been a large-scale exodus from the field and a failure to draw in new applicants.

## Imperatives for Development

The importance of the library and its personnel as a catalyst for growth and change in the nation has not been sufficiently acknowledged or understood:

(a) The redress and equality imperatives that should direct advancements and service delivery in all types of LIS are not being addressed by the library sector's financial resources.
(b) A lack of LIS involvement in government-sponsored development initiatives like Asgisa and Jipsa.
(c) Traditional leaders in rural regions are underutilized in LIS promotion and decision-making, which would greatly boost community involvement and LIS use.
(d) Many individuals, both at the tertiary level and in the industry, lack the reading and informational abilities necessary to properly utilize library services.
(e) A lot of individuals are also ignorant of the advantages libraries offer, such as knowledge of rights, services, health, and jobs.
(f) Poor people use libraries less frequently. Libraries are largely out of the poor's grasp due to their geographic dispersal.

(g) Lack of visibility affects libraries across all industries.

(h) LIS does not offer all the information and services that could help with the eradication of poverty and social cohesion.

(i) LIS can do more to enhance democracy by promoting critical and independent thought.

## The Culture of Reading

The nation has very low levels of information literacy in reading, writing, and other areas:

(a) Libraries play an undervalued role in solving this problem across all sectors.

(b) The absence of information literacy is a big hurdle in the workplace and has a devastating impact on productivity.

(c) The digital gap affects people's capacity for thought and the growth of their brains.

## Indigenous Knowledge Systems

Indigenous knowledge mainstreaming, as well as collecting and disseminating it in book, audio, and video formats have been largely ignored by libraries. In the marketplace, indigenous knowledge is not valued.

## Access to Library Services

The library's services are inaccessible to many people:

(a) Access to library services is not equally distributed geographically among urban and rural areas, suburban areas, formal and informal settlements, provinces, and local governments. Not just for public and school libraries, but also for some university libraries, this is true.

(b) Potential library users have limited access to information and library services due to a dearth and in many cases a total lack, of acceptable resources in their respective languages.

(c) Access is further restricted by staff members' inability to communicate with clients in their native tongues and other languages.

(d) A lot of libraries are located in outdated or non-ideal buildings. Infrastructure construction to allow access to the facilities is challenging.

(e) Many libraries do not provide accessible formats for visually impaired and learning-disabled users.

### Information and Communications Technology

The technology required to support library operations and give users access to electronic material is lacking in many LIS, as is the knowledge of how to use it. The duties of the librarian and the library are changing due to ICT.

### Procurement of Library and Information Resources

Ineffective and wasteful methods make it difficult to acquire library and information resources. Publishers and booksellers who are members of reputable professional organizations and who are totally committed to helping libraries achieve their obligation to their communities are needed to work with LIS as stakeholders in the sector.

## CONCLUSION

The effect of IT Technology on academic libraries is examined in this essay. It draws attention to how university libraries might change to serve a larger and more diverse student body, how open access mandates are implemented and governed, and how traditional librarianship responsibilities are being replaced. In order for libraries to fully benefit from IT Utilities, more funding, commercial collaborations, staff training and skill development opportunities, a larger information exchange, and closer cooperation with other professional organizations are all needed. Together with new business models for collaboration between academic IT services and libraries, shared services between institutions, and cooperative initiatives between the two, rigid impact studies of IT utilities in libraries should be conducted. The new user-centered method of service delivery illustrates how academic libraries can change and advance to meet changing user needs.

## REFERENCES

[1] Applegate, R. (2009). The library is for studying: Student preferences for study space. *The Journal of Academic Librarianship*; 35(4): 341–346.

[2] Arts Council England (2013). Envisioning the library of the future phases 1 and 2: Full report. Arts Council England: London.

[3] Arte, A. and Cassella, M. (2014). Survey on Open Access collection development and management: a comparative analysis between Italy

and UK. Paper presented at IFLA WLIC 2014, 16–22 August, Lyon, France, http://library.ifla.org/845/1/108-arte_en.pdf, accessed 17 June 2016.

[4] Bell, S.J. and Shank, J. (2004). The blended librarian a blueprint for redefining the teaching and learning role of academic librarians. College & Research Libraries News; 65 (7): 372–375.

[5] Ben-Zvi, T. (2010). The efficacy of business simulation games in creating decision support systems: An experimental investigation. Decision Support Systems; 49 (1): 61–69.

[6] Berube, L. (2011). Do You Web 2.0? Public Libraries and Social Networking. Chandos Publishing: Oxford.

[7] Bilandzic, M. and Johnson, D. (2013). Hybrid placemaking in the library: Designing digital technology to enhance users' on-site experience. *The Australian Library Journal,* 62(4): 258–271.

[8] Brewer, E.A. (2002). The consumer side of search". *Communications of the ACM*; 45(9): 40–41.

[9] Cameron, C. and Siddall, G. (2015). Academic staff perceptions and use of reading lists for book ordering. *SCONUL Focus*; 64, 41–44.

[10] Charsky, D. and Ressler, W. (2011). "Games are made for fun": Lessons on the effects of concept maps in the classroom use of computer games. *Computers & Education*, 56(3): 604–615.

[11] Christiansen, L., Stombler, M. and Thaxton, L. (2004). A report on librarian-faculty relations from a sociological perspective. *The Journal of Academic Librarianship,* 30(2): 116–121.

[12] Chu, S.K. and Du, H.S. (2013). Social networking tools for academic libraries. *Journal of Librarianship and Information Science*, 45(1): 64–75.

[13] Clark, C. and Hawkins, L. (2010). Young People's Reading: The Importance of the Home Environment and Family Support. More Findings from Our National Survey. National Literacy Trust, http://eric.ed.gov/?id=ED510272, accessed 17 June 2016.

[14] Cox, A.M. and Pinfield, S. (2014). Research data management and libraries: Current activities and future priorities. *Journal of Librarianship and Information Science*; 46(4): 299–316.

[15] Creed-Dikeogu, G. and Clark, C. (2013). Are you MOOC-ing yet? A review for academic libraries. *Kansas Library Association College and University Libraries Section Proceedings*; 3 (1): 9–13.

[16] Currall, J. and Moss, M. (2008). We are archivists, but are we OK? *Records Management Journal;* 18 (1): 69–91.

[17] Davidson, J., Jones, S. and Molloy, L. (2014). Big data: the potential role of research data management and research data registries. In*:*

*IFLA World Library and Information Congress 80th IFLA General Conference and Assembly,* Lyon, France, 16–22 August, http://eprints.gla.ac.uk/102160/, accessed 17 June 2016.

[18] Datig, I. (2015). Walking in your users' shoes: An introduction to user experience research as a tool for developing user-centered libraries. *College & Undergraduate Libraries;* 22 (3–4): 234–246.

[19] De Castro, P., Shearer, K. and Summann, F. (2014). The gradual merging of repository and CRIS solutions to meet institutional research information management requirements. *Procedia Computer Science;* 33, 39–46.

[20] Deterding, S., Björk, S.L., Nacke, L.E., Dixon, D. and Lawley, E. (2013). Designing gamification: creating gameful and playful experiences, CHI'13 extended abstracts on human factors in computing systems, ACM, 3263, http://dl.acm.org/citation.cfm?id=2479662, accessed 17 June 2016.

[21] Fjällbrant, N. (1997). Scholarly communication-historical development and new possibilities. *IATUL Conference Proceedings, Norwegian University of Science and Technology,* 30 June–4th July, http://www.iatul.org/conference/proceedings/vol07/papers/full/nfpaper.html, accessed 07 March 2016.

[22] Gilmour, R. and Sapp, G. (2002). A brief history of the future of academic libraries: predictions and speculations from the literature of the profession, 1975 to 2000—part one, 1975 to 1989, portal. Libraries and the Academy; 2 (4): 553–576.

[23] Gilmour, R. and Sapp, G. (2003). A brief history of the future of academic libraries: Predictions and speculations from the literature of the profession, 1975 to 2000—part two, 1990 to 2000, portal. *Libraries and the Academy;* 3 (1): 13–34.

[24] Hall, M. (2012). Green or gold? Open access after Finch. Insights; 25 (3): 235–240.

[25] Head, A.J. and Eisenberg, M.B. (2009). Finding context: what today's college students say about conducting research in the digital age. Project information literacy progress report. Project information literacy, http://files.eric.ed.gov/fulltext/ED535161.pdf, accessed 07 March 2016.

[26] Higher Education Funding Council for England (2015). Policy for open access in the post-2014 Research Excellence Framework, http://www.hefce.ac.uk/pubs/year/2014/201407/, accessed 07 March 2016.

[27] Houghton, J.W. and Oppenheim, C. (2010). The economic implycations of alternative publishing models. Prometheus; 28(1): 41–54.

[28] IT as a Utility Network+. (n.d.) About, http://www.itutility.ac.uk/what-is-it-as-a-utility-itaau/, accessed 17 March 2016.

[29] Jacobs, N., Thomas, A. and McGregor, A. (2008). Institutional repositories in the UK: The JISC approach. Library Trends; 57 (2): 124–141.

[30] Kingsley, D.A. and Kennan, M.A. (2015). Open access: The whipping boy for problems in scholarly publishing. *Communications of the Association for Information Systems;* 37(14), http://aisel.aisnet.org/cais/vol37/iss1/14, accessed 17 March 2016.

[31] Liu, Z. (2006). Print vs. electronic resources: A study of user perceptions, preferences, and use. *Information Processing & Management*; 42(2): 583–592.

[32] Martzoukou, K. (2013). Empowering information literacy and continuing professional development of librarians: New paradigms for learning. In: Kurbanoglu S., Grassian E., Mizrachi D., Catts, R. and Špiranec S. (eds). Proceedings of the European Conference on Information Literacy, ECIL 2013. Worldwide Commonalities and Challenges in Information Literacy Research and Practice, Springer: Istanbul, Turkey, 647–654.

[33] Morris, M.R., Teevan, J. and Panovich, K. (2010). What do people ask their social networks, and why?: a survey study of status message q&a behavior, in Proceedings of the SIGCHI Conference on Human Factors in Computing Systems, ACM: 1739, http://131.107.65.14/en-us/um/people/merrie/papers/social_qna_chi2010.pdf, accessed 17 June 2016.

[34] National Literacy Trust. (2013) Children's on-screen reading overtakes reading inprint, http://www.literacytrust.org.uk/media/5371_children_s_on-screen_reading overtakes reading_in_print, accessed 07 March 2016.

[35] Nicholas, D., Rowlands, I., Jubb, M. and Jamali, H.R. (2010). The impact of the economic downturn on libraries: with special reference to university libraries. The Journal of Academic Librarianship; 36(5): 376–382.

[36] Nicholson, S. (2013). Two paths to motivation through game design elements: reward-based gamification and meaningful gamification, Conference2013 Proceedings, https://www.ideals.illinois.edu/bitstream/handle/2142/42082/313.pdf?sequence=2accessed 17 June 2016.

# Libraries Contribute Across the Sustainable Development Goals Using BigData

**Asha Negi[1] and Sanjiv K. Sain[2]**

## Abstract

In order to contribute to sustainable development goals, this research paper evaluates how big data is used in libraries (SDGs). It begins with a description of big data's significance and promise before concentrating on how new developments in the field are having an impact on libraries. Additionally, it investigates how much the SDGs are taken into consideration in strategic planning for libraries and how library staff members feel their efforts are influencing the SDGs. The most crucial information is that library personnel are aware of the SDGs, they are involved in the long-term planning, which of the five SDGs specifically listed they believe libraries have influenced the most, and they are aware of the SDGs. How frequently have the libraries been involved in initiatives to encourage the five SDGs that have been focused on? What initiatives are library employees pursuing to advance the five SDGs that have been highlighted? Inadequate technical infrastructure, a lack of new task-specific skills, problems with open data legislation, a lack of government and library collaboration, a lack of LIS workers' enthusiasm, and a lack of ambition are all problems associated with this data flood. Libraries must form a collaboration with governments, make access and privacy-related taxonomies, increase literacy in information and aggressively intensify their advocacy for information freedom while balancing it with the protection of individual privacy in order to deal with the new roles and expectations. They must also advocate for policy reform. The libraries have so much potential for the development of these sustainable development goals.

[1] Research Scholar, Himalayiya University Dehradun, India.
Library Assistant, DIT University, Dehradun, India.
E-mail: negi6395788819@gmail.com

[2] Research Scholar, Himalayiya University Dehradun, India.
Librarian, DIT University, Dehradun, India.
E-mail: sanjivsain74@gmail.com

*Keywords: BigData, UN, Global Development Agenda, Sustainable Development Goals, Information Specialists, OCLC.*

## INTRODUCTION

The "UN's Sustainable Development Goals (SDGs)" are shaped in large part by libraries. "OCLC conducted an online poll of library personnel globally" to find out how library operations impacted the SDGs. They believed that libraries may have the biggest impact on the following five SDGs: Quality Education, Decent Employment and Economic Development, Reduced Inequality, Peace, Justice, Strong Institutions, and Partnerships for the Goals. Examples of how libraries support the SDGs include the Global Fund to Fight AIDS, Tuberculosis, and Malaria, the UN Millennium Project, the repetition of ODA to Africa by the G8, the MDG Africa Navigation Group, and the 2008 global financial crisis. These exercises can assist library employees in making the most of their institution's contribution to sustainable development and informing their strategic planning.

Libraries, which act as information centers, have become the focus of worldwide attention as a result of the creative breakthroughs generated by big data in almost every industry. This is a result of recent changes in information and communication technology, particularly the widespread adoption of digital technologies and their use in workplaces and personal life, which has caused a sharp increase in the volume and variety of digital data. According to Cisco and the World Economic Forum, "billions of people's interactions with digital devices generate a flood of data every day, and online or mobile financial transactions, social media traffic, and GPS coordinates now generate over 2.5 quintillion bytes of so-called "big data" every day". According to Michael and Miller, "data mining has existed since people began keeping records in the modern era, but big data brings together not only large amounts of data but also various data types that were never considered together previously".

## THE 2030 AGENDA FOR SUSTAINABLE DEVELOPMENT ERA

"The 2030 Agenda for Sustainable Development" is a "new global development framework centered on 17 Sustainable Development Goals (SDGs), which cover topics such as natural resource management, sustainable consumption and production, effective institutions, good governance, the rule of law, and peaceful societies. The overarching goal is poverty eradication, and access to information is critical". Big data has the ability to encourage participatory development by giving everyone the tools they need to assert their rights and handle their own developmental issues. Scientific opportunities arise from the identification of previously unobservable patterns.

Figure 1: A Summary of the Sustainable Development Goals (SDGs)

## Big Data

The definition of "big data" is up for debate. For the first time in 2013, the "Oxford English Dictionary" included the term "big data" in its online update to refer "to extremely large data sets that can be computationally analyzed to reveal patterns, trends, and associations, particularly relating to human behavior and interactions". According to Boyd and Crawford (2012), "big data is a cultural, technological, and scholarly phenomenon based on the interaction of technology, analysis, and mythology". Douglas Laney's 2001 "big data framework based on the three V's (volume, variety, and velocity) appears more appropriate given that these characteristics reflect large amounts of various types of data, both structured and unstructured, arriving at a fast and constant pace, necessitating real-time analytics to derive meaningful information and knowledge". De Mauro, Greco, and Grimaldi examined "a large number of industry and academic articles on big data and discovered that the main themes of big data were "information, technology, methods, and impact," and thus defined the term as an information asset with such high volume, velocity, and variety that it necessitates specific technology and analytical methods for its transformation into value."

## The Contribution of Libraries in Achieving the SDGs

It has long been understood how important libraries are to the cause of world progress. According to the "International Federation of Library Associations" (IFLA), "access to information is crucial to attaining the SDGs, and libraries are already contributing to the progress towards fulfilling the 17 Goals." Libraries in developing countries have received funding from international information professional organizations like IFLA and EIFL to provide access to electronic resources and instruction in ICT. Digital gadgets, library management systems, e-resources, and the use of social media to engage users are just a few examples of the technological innovations that have helped libraries in Singapore find new methods to meet community needs. Findings, discoveries, inventions, practical knowledge, scholarship, and research—all of which are crucial to achieving a nation's objectives—are stored in libraries.

"The National Library of South Africa (NLSA)" operates "a network of delivery sites for government programs and services, preserving cultural heritage and fostering social cohesion". In Botswana, "public libraries have taken steps to support government objectives such as introducing ICT access, improving computer skills, and enabling users to be successful in business, education, and employment". In Uganda, "the National Library of Uganda (NLU) offers ICT training to female farmers", "Kitengesa Community Library offers similar programs", and "Makerere University offers health information literacy to health professionals and local communities". Despite the fact that the current digital environment has fundamentally altered not only libraries and information services but also the responsibilities and expectations of information professionals, a review of the literature shows that libraries and information professionals are crucial to the 2030 global development agenda.

## Big Data's Effects on Libraries' Contribution to Reaching the SDGs

The big data revolution is changing the role of libraries in many ways.

### *A New Role in Managing Research Data*

Due to the data flood caused by computation and networks, libraries are reinventing their position and role in the ecosystem of digital academic communication. Organizing big data resources requires collaboration, but making sense of all the data requires time, according to Patrick

Morehead of Future Research and Analysis. As experts in the ontology work required to produce the metadata that powers big data analytics applications, libraries have an edge. Ex Libris Alma has been a focus of Roger Brisson's work at the Boston University Library as he attempts to overcome the difficulties associated with scholarly inquiry and intellectual exchange.

## Curation of Data

Many new applications for library data have been made possible by the emergence of linked data, including text and data mining, digital preservation, web archiving, digitization, and management of online resources. As a result of big data technologies like data storage, parallel computing, predictive analytics, and machine learning, which guarantee better performance and instruments for improvement, libraries will be able to use and curate data in unique and creative ways. Three of the most crucial big data projects for librarians are user studies, collection use analysis, and cross-disciplinary comparison research, according to Huwe (2014). The Las Vegas-Clark County Library District Foundation uses analytics through the CIVIC technologies service to better understand the populations it serves. Ten libraries already use a big data analytics service to study usage patterns and trends.

### *Developing Taxonomies*

Because data from digitization programs, digital research, and the social web is so complicated, librarians should be involved in the taxonomy-building process.

### *Libraries as Innovation Hotspots*

To address SDG goal 9, libraries have implemented new innovations. "North Carolina State University's Hunt Library serves as a technology incubator, and the Los Angeles Public Library hosted the Immigration Hackathon". "The Institute of Museum and Library Services (IMLS) has invested in an e-reader app as well as tools and services to assist the public in gaining access to eBooks and other digital content". "Literacy Bridge used the Talking Book to close gender and literacy gaps."Small Business Enterprises (SMEs) can be helped in overcoming big data utilization barriers by a facilitated knowledge management approach that uses filtered big data.

Big data is being used in higher education to improve student learning outcomes and expand access to high-quality education opportunities. Information specialists are experts at analyzing circulation figures, database logins, as well as other transactional data, to assess their applicability to student development. The modern digital library has extended beyond its conventional focus on metadata, bibliographic, and authority data to handle or interact with a wide variety of data types. By filling in the information gap between what the general public knows and what can be done with the data acquired from them, public libraries may help people better understand this new digital world.

A library is a repository where people can go to ask questions, consult with experts, and use metadata. Fast-developing nations of the south are facing the same demanding situations as the commercial north, and this has consequences for the scale and role of 'useful resource'. Libraries are critical for achieving the SDGs because they provide information on basic rights and entitlements, public services, the environment, health, education, job opportunities, and government spending. However, as home internet use increases, library internet use will decline. The OECD/DAC and beneficiary countries are debating how to capture these additional financial flows and the implications for ODA.

## Initiatives for Open Data and Open Access

In order to feel more at ease with emerging technological trends, libraries and librarians have welcomed open data projects. As a result, libraries cheered when President Obama signed an executive order promoting the use of open data. Jeff Jonas, an IBMS data expert, suggests listening to the data as it "speaks to you" in order to evaluate enormous volumes of data and find connections, which are essential for decision- and policy-makers.

## Big Data Challenges for Libraries in Developing Countries

Because it includes gathering personal data and information, Big data presents significant security risks to individuals, organizations, and governments. Most developing countries still lack adequate data protection and privacy laws, and a lack of infrastructure makes it difficult to gather and evaluate data. "Hilbert (2013) argues that the extraction of actionable knowledge from the vast amounts of available digital information is the natural next step in the evolution from the "Information Age" to the "Knowledge Age". However, in developing countries, the diffusion process is hampered by a lack of infrastructure, human capital, economic resource availability, and institutional frameworks, resulting in a new dimension of the digital divide." According to scholars such as "Grayling and Zulu (2010) and Kwanya (2014), African libraries and information centers are ill-equipped to contribute meaningfully to the current global digital knowledge economy. Due to a lack of motivation, government policies, financial constraints, and expertise, libraries face challenges in implementing Vision 2030."

"The OCLC Global Council and the Sustainable Development Goals (SDGs) have joined forces to assist libraries in promoting and improving their best concepts. The five SDGs were Quality Education (SDG 4), Decent Work and Economic Growth (SDG 8), Reduced Inequalities (SDG 10), Peace, Justice, and Strong Institutions (SDG 16), and Partnerships for the Goals (SDG 17). (SDG 17)." Library staff viewed quality education as the most important goal, but SDG activity varied by region and type.

The OCLC Global Council focuses on the five SDGs from the UN SDGs beneficial to where libraries have the greatest impact are:

### SDG 4: Quality Education

"A plan of action for people, planet, and prosperity," according to the "2030 Agenda for Sustainable Development. There are 17 Sustainable Development Goals included (SDGs). These goals, which include economic, social, and environmental considerations, are inextricably linked." To "provide inclusive and equitable quality education and encourage lifelong learning opportunities for all," according to SDG4, which focuses on education. According to "Goal 4 of the Sustainable Development Goals, all people should have access to inclusive, equitable, and high-quality education (SDGs). With 260 million children not enrolled in school in 2018, equivalent to one-fifth of all children worldwide, UNICEF works with governments to improve the quality and inclusiveness of schools. Indicator 4.2.1 counts the number of children (aged 24–59 months) All girls and boys should have equal access to free, equitable, and high-quality primary and secondary education, technical/vocational and higher education, relevant skills for decent work, gender equality and inclusion, universal youth literacy, and education for sustainable development and global citizenship by 2030. Effective learning environments, scholarships, and teachers and educators are three methods of implementation."

### Lifelong Learning, Equality, and Participation

Libraries provide everyone with access to education and opportunities for lifelong learning, and some are directly linking their activities and programs to the SDGs. Solar SPELL, an Arizona State University project, is a mobile digital library that generates its own Wi-Fi hotspot. Solar SPELL team members travel to developing countries to teach Peace Corps volunteers, teachers, and healthcare professionals how to use Solar SPELL libraries to develop 21st-century skills in offline settings.

A full and productive life for every person as well as sustainable development depends on access to high-quality education and opportunities for lifelong learning. Millions of youngsters are still not enrolled in school despite tremendous progress in that direction, especially in places where educational infrastructure is having a hard time keeping up with population expansion. Quality education is hampered by inadequate classroom resources and school infrastructure. More efforts are needed to target disadvantaged communities in Sub-Saharan Africa and Southern Asia in order to attain this goal. 263 million children, teenagers, and young people were not attending school in 2014, with the majority of them residing in Southern Asia and Sub-Saharan Africa. According to "parity indices, children and adolescents from the richest 20% of households performed better in reading than those from the poorest 20%. Girls outperformed boys in reading proficiency at the end of primary and lower secondary school."

### *SDG 8: Decent Work and Economic Growth*

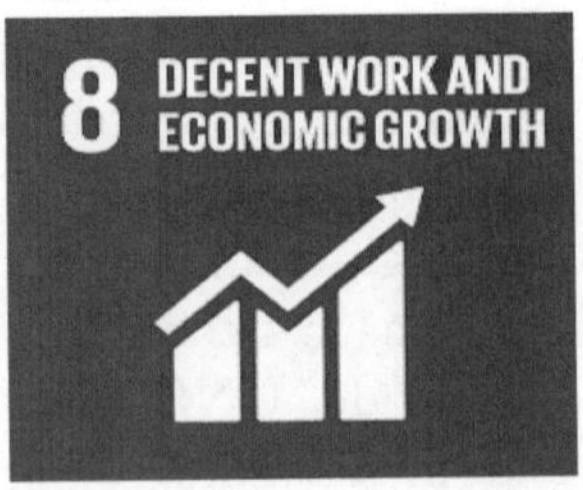


"The United Nations Sustainable Development Goals (SDGs) are pushing governments, individuals, universities, and businesses to change their ways in order to meet benchmarks and secure a sustainable future by 2030." "SDG 8 focuses on promoting long-term and inclusive economic growth, full and productive employment, and decent work for all. Spectra Force is a multi-award-winning global staffing and consulting firm that has developed and implemented ground-breaking talent-sourcing technologies to attract top-tier talent candidates."

### *SDG 10: Reduced Inequality*

The world's inequalities remain stark, with the richest 5% capturing 44% of global income. Between 1990 and 2010, income inequality in developing countries increased by 11%. Divorced women are more than twice as likely as divorced men to be poor, and gender inequalities affect income as well as other basic aspects of well-being. Through advocacy and public programs, UN Women strives to reduce inequality.

### *SDG 16: Peace, Justice and Strong Institutions*

Peace, justice, and strong institutions" is the focus of "Sustainable Development Goal 16." One of the 17 Sustainable Development Goals established by the United Nations in 2015, its official formulation is to "promote peaceful and inclusive societies for sustainable development, ensure access to justice for all, and promote effective, accountable, and inclusive institutions at all levels." "To achieve the Goal by 2030, 12 targets must be met. There will be 23 indicators used to track progress toward goals. There are ten in the objective. Reduce violence, promote rule of law, reduce illicit financial and arms flows, recover stolen assets, reduce corruption, develop effective institutions, provide legal identity, ensure public access to information, protect fundamental freedoms, and enforce non-discriminatory laws and policies for sustainable development."

### *SDG 17: Partnerships for the Goals*

To achieve success, "the UN Sustainable Development Goals (SDGs) emphasize the importance of global partnerships and cooperation. Universities contribute to the SDGs by collaborating with other countries, promoting best practices, and publishing data." "The Office of Public Engagement at the University of Minnesota will launch an interactive system in 2020 to help communicate the University's public impact. Sustainable development Goal 17 aims to empower developing-country sectors and businesses by improving energy, infrastructure, transportation systems, and IT infrastructure."

## Overview of the Literature on the Influence of Libraries on the SDGs

Libraries are critical to achieving Sustainable Development Goals (SDGs). Ending hunger, fostering innovation, and providing conservation education are examples of how they have impacted all 17 SDGs. They are critical for fostering social capital and bringing members of a community together, as well as creating digital inclusion and providing access to information and information literacy. "OCLC conducted a survey to identify library activities that can help to advance the SDGs, as well as how they are being considered and integrated into library strategic planning."

## CONCLUSIONS

The SDGs have a large deal of potential contribution from big data, but its implications for the function of libraries have not yet been thoroughly understood. According to Literate, there is a disparity between developed and poor nations when it comes to the adoption of big data projects, with libraries in wealthy nations participating in these programs to a greater extent. All parties involved in the gathering, the creation of tools and strategies that enable the use of big data for SDG achievement, and ongoing professional development are required for this. The most precious resource, "information and knowledge," which guides decisions for sustainable growth, can only be delivered by libraries. Only those with Internet access, social media accounts or connections to library employees via professional virtual networks were eligible for this study. The results provide information about the activities that library staff is conducting, and the respondents' perception of the impact these activities have on the SDGs. This research builds on the writing of "Edwards (2018) who encourages all libraries to link their work to the global agenda as a way to demonstrate their value. Further research is needed to identify how library staff integrates the SDGs into their planning and how they develop activities to support the SDGs, and how these contributions can be evaluated to assess their impact on this ecosystem. Identifying and articulating the role the library can play in advancing and impacting the SDGs to demonstrate libraries' value within the larger ecosystem is an important next step."This paper suggests that the form of understanding desirable to manipulate information is simply establishment to materialize inside librarians' positions and that the inspirations of SDGs at the sporting of people would be fine, thoughtful and enormous.

## REFERENCES

[1] Amunga, H.A. (2011). Information literacy inside the twenty-first-century universities: The Kenyan experience.

[2] Banisa, D. (2015). Access to Information Central to the Post-2015 Development Agenda. *International Federation of Library Associations & Institutions.*

[3] Bays, J. (2014). Harnessing Big Data to cope with the arena's issues. Retrieved January 20, 2017, from http://voices.Mckinseyonsociety.Com/harnessingbig-statistics-to-deal with-the-worlds-troubles

[4] Bell, S. (2013). Promise and troubles of massive facts. Library Journal. Bieraugel, M. (2013). Keeping up with big statistics. Retrieved January 2, 2017, from Association of College and Research Libraries: http://www.Ala.Org/acrl/guides/keeping_up_with/big_data

[5] Boyd, D. and Crawford, K. (2012).Critical questions for large facts: Provocations for a cultural, technological and scholarly phenomenon. *Information, Communication & Society*, 15(five), 662–679.

[6] Bradley, F. (2016). An international with familiar literacy: The position of libraries and get admission to facts in the UN 2030 timetable. IFLA Journal, forty-two, 118-one hundred twenty-five.

[7] Chen, C.P. and Zhang, C.-Y. (2014). Data-in-depth programs, challenges, strategies and technology: A survey on big records. *Information Sciences,* 275, 314–347.

[8] Chen, H., Chiang, R.H. and Storey, V.C. (2012). Business intelligence and analytics: From large data to large effect. MIS Quarterly, 36(4), 1165-1188.

[9] De Mauro, A., Greco, M. and Grimaldi, M. (2016). A formal definition of Big Data based on its essential features. *Library Review*, 65(3), 122-135.

[10] Diebold, F.X. (2012). On the Origin (s) and Development of the Term 'Big Data'. The University of Pennsylvania, Department of Economics. Philadelphia: SSRN.

[11] Echezona, R.I., Ozioko, R.E. and Ugwuanyi, C.F. (2011). Public library intervention in conflict resolutions in the iger Delta region of Nigeria:

Librarian's perspectives. *International Journal of Library and Information Science,* 3(2), 98-106.

[12] Elbert, M., Fuegi, D. and Lipeikaite, U. (2012). Public libraries in Africa—agents for development and innovation? Current perceptions of local stakeholders. IFLA, 38(2), 148–165.

[13] Fourie, I. and Meyer, A. (2016). The role of libraries in developing and informed and educated nation. Library Hi Tech, 34(3), 422–432.

[14] Frederick, D.E. (2016). Libraries, data and the fourth industrial revolution (Data Deluge Column). Library Hi Tech News, 33(5), 9–12.

[15] Gandomi, A. and Haider, M. (2015). Beyond the hype: Big data concepts, methods, and analytics. *International Journal of Information Management*, 35(2), 37–144.

(a) Global Pulse (2016). Measuring Poverty with Machine Roof Counting. Retrieved October 26, 2016, from United Nations Global Pulse: http://www.unglobalpulse.org/projects/measuring-poverty-machine-roof-counting

(b) Greeley, M., Lucas, H., Chai, J. and Cummins, M. (2013). Introduction: real-time monitoring for the most vulnerable–investing in common guidance for equity and quality. IDS Bulletin, 44(2), 1–14.

(c) Huwe, T. (2014). Big data and the library: A natural fit. Computers in Libraries, 34(2), 17–18.

(d) IFLA (2012). How Libraries contribute to sustainable development & the SDGs: Impact report. *International Federation of Library Associations & Institutions.*

(e) IFLA (2013). Access to Information Central to the Post-2015 Development Agenda. Retrieved October 15, 2016, from IFLA.

(f) IFLA (2014). The Lyon Declaration Tackles Information Access and Sustainable Development. Retrieved October 26, 2016, from Information Today: http://www.lyondeclaration.org/content/pages/lyon-declaration.pdf

(g) IFLA (2015). Access and Opportunity for All: How Libraries Contribute to the United Nations 2030 Agenda. International Federation of Library Associations and Institutions (IFLA).

(h) Kayode, D.S. (2016). The role of the library in achieving Vision 2030 Goals. *CEC Journal,* 4(2), 1–5.

# Impact of ICT on Library System

**S.P. Gupta***

***Abstract***

The impact of Information and Communication Technology (ICT) on libraries today has been profound. Libraries have experienced significant changes in the way they operate, deliver services, and interact with their users due to the integration of ICT. With the help of ICT, libraries have been able to provide efficient and effective services to their users. Digitization of library collections, e-resources, digital preservation, digital reference services, and library management systems are some examples of how libraries have incorporated ICT in their services. The integration of ICT has transformed libraries into digital hubs where users can access information from anywhere at any time. This has resulted in increased access to information, enhanced user experiences, and improved library services. Despite the benefits of ICT, there are also challenges such as the need for staff training and funding to keep up with the ever-evolving technology. Nevertheless, the impact of ICT on libraries today is undeniable, and it is expected to continue to shape the future of libraries.

***Keywords:*** *Information and Communication Technology (ICT), The New York Public Library (NYPL),.*

## INTRODUCTION

ICT (Information Communication Technologies) is mostly similar as IT but it is mostly used as to represent a broader category of everything related to computer and digital technologies.

The way we think about how a library should be has changed with times. At present with the help of technological advances and how easily it can be accessed anywhere in the world.

Information and Communication Technology (ICT) has had a significant impact on library systems, making them more efficient,

* Deputy Librarian, XLRI Institute, Jamshedpur, India.
E-mail: shankarxlri@gmai.com

effective, and accessible. Some of the ways ICT has impacted library systems include:

1. **Automation of Library Functions:** ICT has enabled libraries to automate many of their core functions such as cataloguing, circulation, and reference services.
2. **Digitization of Collections:** Libraries can now digitize their collections, making them accessible to a wider audience and preserving them for future generations.
3. **Virtual Reference Services:** The use of ICT has made it possible for libraries to offer virtual reference services, enabling users to access information and receive assistance from anywhere in the world.
4. **Mobile Access:** With the increasing use of mobile devices, ICT has made it possible for users to access library resources and services from anywhere, at any time.
5. **Improved User Experience:** ICT has enabled libraries to provide a more intuitive and user-friendly experience, making it easier for users to find and access the information they need.

Overall, ICT has had a profound impact on the way libraries operate and has enabled them to better serve their communities.

Information and Communication Technology (ICT) has greatly impacted the way libraries function, leading to the development of digital libraries. Here is a case study of how ICT has been implemented in a library:

## Case Study: New York Public Library

The New York Public Library (NYPL) is one of the largest public library systems in the United States. It has implemented various ICT solutions to enhance its services and meet the needs of its patrons. Some of these include:

- **Digital Collection:** NYPL has made its collections, including books, manuscripts, maps, photographs, and more, available online. Users can access over 800,000 digital items, including e-books, through the NYPL digital library.
- **Online Reference Services:** NYPL provides online reference services to its patrons, which allows them to ask questions and receive answers from librarians 24/7.
- **Mobile Apps:** NYPL has developed mobile apps for both iOS and Android devices that allow users to search the library's catalog,

access its digital collections, and receive recommendations based on their reading history.

- **Technology Training Programs:** NYPL offers technology training programs to help patrons learn how to use ICT tools and resources, such as e-readers, tablets, and computers.
- **Wi-Fi Access:** NYPL provides free Wi-Fi access to its patrons, allowing them to connect to the internet and access online resources while inside the library.

The implementation of ICT solutions has greatly improved the services offered by NYPL, making it easier for patrons to access information and resources. The digital collection and online reference services have also made the library's collections more accessible to a wider audience, including people with disabilities or those who live in remote areas.

Overall, the NYPL case study demonstrates how ICT can be used to modernize and enhance library services, making them more accessible and user-friendly for patrons.

## Role of ICT in Library Services

Information and Communication Technology (ICT) has revolutionized the way library services are delivered. Here are some key roles of ICT in library services:

1. **Access to Information:** ICT has enabled libraries to provide access to a vast range of electronic resources such as e-books, e-journals, and online databases. This has increased the scope and depth of information that can be accessed by library users, irrespective of their location and time.
2. **Digital Preservation:** Libraries are using ICT tools to preserve and manage their digital collections, including images, videos, audio recordings, and other digital assets. This ensures the long-term availability of digital content for future generations.
3. **Online Catalogue and Circulation System:** ICT has enabled libraries to automate their cataloguing and circulation systems. This includes online catalogues, which make it easier for users to search and locate materials, and online circulation systems, which enable users to borrow and return materials remotely.
4. **Virtual Reference Services:** With the advent of ICT, libraries can provide virtual reference services to users. This includes online chat,

email, and video conferencing services, which enable users to get assistance from librarians remotely.

5. **E-learning and Research Support:** Libraries can support e-learning and research by providing online tutorials, research guides, and other resources that help users to acquire new skills and conduct research effectively.
6. **Digital Collaboration:** ICT tools have made it easier for libraries to collaborate with other institutions and organizations. This includes sharing resources, developing joint collections, and collaborating on research projects.

In summary, ICT has transformed library services by expanding the range and depth of resources available to users, enabling virtual reference services, automating library systems, preserving digital collections, supporting e-learning and research, and facilitating digital collaboration.

## ICT based Library Services

ICT-based library services refer to library services that use Information and Communication Technology (ICT) to enhance the delivery of services to library users. Here are some examples of ICT-based library services:

1. **Online Catalogue:** An online catalogue is a searchable database of library holdings that allows users to search for library materials remotely. Users can access the catalogue from anywhere at any time and can search for materials by author, title, subject, or keyword.
2. **E-books and E-Journals:** Many libraries now offer electronic versions of books and journals that can be accessed remotely by library users. This service allows users to access materials even when the library is closed or when they are not physically in the library.
3. **Virtual Reference Services:** With virtual reference services, users can contact librarians via email, chat, or video conferencing to get assistance remotely. This service enables users to get help with their research or to ask questions about library services without physically visiting the library.
4. **Online Circulation System:** An online circulation system allows library users to borrow and return materials remotely. This service enables users to renew their borrowed items and to place holds on items that are checked out.

5. **Research and Instruction Support:** Many libraries now offer online research and instruction support services. These services include online tutorials, research guides, and other resources that help users to acquire new skills and conduct research effectively.
6. **Digital Preservation:** ICT can help libraries to preserve their digital collections. Libraries can use digital preservation tools to ensure that digital materials are preserved for future generations.
7. **Social Media:** Many libraries now use social media platforms to engage with library users. Social media is used to promote library services, events, and new acquisitions. It also enables library users to interact with librarians and other library users.

In summary, ICT-based library services provide greater convenience and accessibility for library users. These services enhance the ability of libraries to deliver services to users, promote their resources and collections, and support learning and research.

## IMPACT OF ICT TOOLS & ACADEMIC LIBRARY

The impact of Information and Communication Technology (ICT) tools on academic libraries has been significant in recent years. Here are some key impacts of ICT on academic libraries:

1. **Access to Information:** ICT tools have enabled academic libraries to provide access to a vast range of electronic resources such as e-books, e-journals, and online databases. This has increased the scope and depth of information that can be accessed by library users, irrespective of their location and time.
2. **Digital Preservation:** ICT tools have helped academic libraries to preserve and manage their digital collections, including images, videos, audio recordings, and other digital assets. This ensures the long-term availability of digital content for future generations.
3. **Online Catalogue and Circulation System:** ICT has enabled academic libraries to automate their cataloguing and circulation systems. This includes online catalogues, which make it easier for users to search and locate materials, and online circulation systems, which enable users to borrow and return materials remotely.
4. **E-Learning and Research Support:** Academic libraries can support e-learning and research by providing online tutorials, research guides, and other resources that help students to acquire new skills and conduct research effectively.

5. **Collaborative Learning:** ICT tools have enabled academic libraries to support collaborative learning by providing online discussion forums, group study rooms, and other collaborative learning tools. This enables students to work together on projects, share information, and learn from one another.
6. **Social Media:** Many academic libraries now use social media platforms to engage with students and faculty members. Social media is used to promote library services, events, and new acquisitions. It also enables library users to interact with librarians and other library users.

In summary, ICT has had a significant impact on academic libraries by enhancing the ability of libraries to deliver services to users, promoting their resources and collections, supporting learning and research, and enabling collaborative learning.

## ICT Skills and Academic Libraries

Information and Communication Technology (ICT) skills are critical for academic libraries to provide effective and efficient services to their users. Here are some of the key ICT skills that are important for academic libraries:

1. **Database Searching:** Academic libraries provide access to a variety of electronic resources such as databases, online journals, and e-books. It is essential for library staff to have strong database searching skills to help users find the information they need.
2. **Online Catalogue Searching:** Library staff need to have strong online catalogue searching skills to help users locate books and other materials in the library. This includes advanced search techniques, as well as knowledge of subject headings and classification systems.
3. **Technical Support:** Academic libraries use a variety of hardware and software to deliver services to users. Library staff need to have strong technical skills to maintain and troubleshoot hardware and software problems.
4. **E-Learning and Research Support:** Academic libraries provide e-learning and research support to their users. Library staff need to have strong skills in instructional design, as well as knowledge of e-learning and research technologies.
5. **Social Media Management:** Many academic libraries use social media platforms to engage with students and faculty members.

Library staff need to have strong skills in social media management, including content creation, social media analytics, and community management.

6. **Digital Preservation:** Academic libraries are increasingly managing digital collections, which requires staff to have skills in digital preservation, metadata management, and digital asset management.

In summary, ICT skills are critical for academic libraries to provide effective and efficient services to their users. Library staff need to have strong skills in database searching, online catalogue searching, technical support, e-learning and research support, social media management, and digital preservation. These skills help to ensure that academic libraries can provide the best possible services to their users.

## ICT and Electronic Library

ICT (Information and Communication Technology) and electronic libraries are closely related concepts.

An electronic library is a digital library that provides access to a collection of digital resources, such as e-books, e-journals, audio and video recordings, and other multimedia content. Electronic libraries are typically accessible via the internet and can be accessed from any device with an internet connection.

ICT refers to the use of technology to communicate, store, and process information. In the context of electronic libraries, ICT is the underlying technology that makes it possible to create and access digital content. This includes hardware such as computers, mobile devices, and servers, as well as software such as databases, digital content management systems, and search engines.

ICT is essential for the effective functioning of electronic libraries. It enables libraries to provide access to a vast amount of digital content from anywhere in the world, which greatly expands the scope of their collections. ICT also makes it easier for libraries to manage their collections, as digital resources can be easily catalogued, searched, and retrieved.

In summary, electronic libraries and ICT are interdependent concepts, with ICT providing the technological infrastructure that makes it possible to create and access digital content, and electronic libraries providing a platform for accessing and managing that content.

## Digital Library Advantages and Disadvantages

Digital libraries have become increasingly popular in recent years, offering a number of advantages over traditional libraries. However, like any technology, they also have some drawbacks. Let's take a look at the advantages and disadvantages of digital libraries in detail.

## Advantages of Digital Libraries

1. **Access:** Digital libraries offer users around-the-clock access to an extensive collection of digital resources. Users can access digital libraries from anywhere in the world, at any time, as long as they have an internet connection. This makes it possible for people to access information even if they live in remote areas or cannot visit a physical library.
2. **Convenience:** Digital libraries are incredibly convenient for users. They eliminate the need to travel to a physical location, saving users time and money. Users can access digital resources from any device with an internet connection, including laptops, tablets, and smartphones.
3. **Search Ability:** Digital libraries make it easy to search for and find specific resources. Users can search by title, author, keyword, or subject, which can save time and effort.
4. **Sustainability:** Digital libraries are more environmentally friendly than traditional libraries since they don't require the printing of physical books or journals. This helps to reduce carbon emissions and conserve resources.
5. **Preservation:** Digital libraries can help to preserve rare and fragile materials that might be difficult to access or prone to damage. By digitizing these materials, libraries can ensure that they are preserved for future generations.

## Disadvantages of Digital Libraries

1. **Access to Technology:** Digital libraries require access to a computer or other internet-enabled device, as well as a reliable internet connection. This can be a barrier for some people, particularly those in remote or low-income areas.
2. **Cost:** Setting up and maintaining a digital library can be costly. Libraries must invest in hardware, software, and digital resources.

This can make it difficult for smaller libraries to create and maintain a digital collection.

3. **Copyright Issues:** Digital libraries must comply with copyright laws, which can be complex and time-consuming. This can make it difficult for libraries to digitize certain materials, such as works that are still under copyright protection.
4. **Technical Issues:** Like any technology, digital libraries can experience technical issues, such as server downtime or data loss. This can disrupt access to digital resources and create frustration for users.
5. **Information Overload:** With the vast amount of information available in digital libraries, it can be easy for users to become overwhelmed. Users may have difficulty sifting through the information to find what they need.

In summary, digital libraries offer numerous advantages in terms of access, convenience, searchability, sustainability, and preservation. However, they also have some disadvantages, such as access to technology, cost, copyright issues, technical issues, and information overload. Despite these drawbacks, digital libraries are likely to continue to grow in popularity as technology advances and more resources become available digitally.

## Hybrid and Digital Library

A hybrid digital and virtual library is a type of library that combines the benefits of digital and virtual libraries. This type of library typically has a physical location where users can access physical books and other materials, but it also offers digital resources that can be accessed online.

In a hybrid library, users can access both physical and digital materials through a single interface, such as a library website or digital catalog. This makes it easy for users to search for and find materials, regardless of their format. For example, users can search for a book and see whether it is available in the physical library or as an e-book that can be accessed online.

A hybrid digital and virtual library can offer a number of advantages to users, including:

1. **Flexibility:** Users can choose whether to access resources physically or digitally, depending on their preferences and needs. This can make it easier for users to access materials when and where they need them.

2. **Access:** A hybrid library can offer users access to a wide range of materials, including physical books, e-books, audio and video recordings, and other digital resources. This can expand the scope of the library's collection and make it easier for users to find what they need.
3. **Convenience:** A hybrid library can be more convenient for users, as they can access materials from anywhere, at any time. This can eliminate the need to travel to a physical location and save users time and money.
4. **Personalization:** A hybrid library can offer users personalized recommendations based on their reading history and interests. This can help users discover new materials that they might not have found otherwise.

However, there are also some challenges and drawbacks to creating and maintaining a hybrid library. These can include:

1. **Cost:** Creating and maintaining a hybrid library can be costly, as it requires both physical and digital infrastructure, as well as a dedicated staff to manage both aspects of the library.
2. **Technology:** A hybrid library requires a robust technology infrastructure to support digital resources and access. This can require ongoing investments in hardware, software, and staff training.
3. **Copyright Issues:** A hybrid library must comply with copyright laws, which can be complex and time-consuming. This can make it difficult for libraries to offer certain materials in a digital format.
4. **User Adoption:** Users may be hesitant to adopt new digital tools or processes, which can make it difficult for the library to fully realize the benefits of a hybrid model.

In summary, a hybrid digital and virtual library offers a flexible and accessible approach to library services, but it also requires significant investments in technology, staff, and resources. Ultimately, the success of a hybrid library depends on the ability of the library to balance the benefits and challenges of both physical and digital resources.

## Online vs. Traditional Library

Online libraries and traditional libraries are two different ways to access and use library resources. Here are some of the differences between the two:

### *Online Library*

1. **Access:** Online libraries can be accessed from anywhere with an internet connection, making it convenient for users to access the resources they need.
2. **Searchability:** Online libraries typically have powerful search tools that make it easy to find specific resources quickly.
3. **Availability:** Online libraries are available 24/7, which means users can access resources whenever they need them.
4. **Diversity:** Online libraries often have a wider range of resources available, including e-books, articles, and other digital materials.
5. **Sustainability:** Online libraries are environmentally friendly since they don't require printing or shipping of physical materials.

### *Traditional Library*

1. **Atmosphere:** Traditional libraries offer a quiet and studious atmosphere, which can be helpful for users who need to concentrate.
2. **Assistance:** Traditional libraries have librarians and staff on hand to help users navigate resources and find the information they need.
3. **Experience:** Traditional libraries provide a more hands-on and sensory experience, allowing users to browse and handle physical materials.
4. **Community:** Traditional libraries can be a hub of activity and provide a sense of community for users.
5. **Access to Rare Materials:** Traditional libraries often have collections of rare and unique materials that may not be available in online libraries.

In summary, online libraries are convenient, accessible, and offer a wide range of digital resources, while traditional libraries offer a more tactile, social, and personalized experience with access to rare materials. Both types of libraries have their own advantages and disadvantages, and the best choice depends on the individual user's needs and preferences.

## Implementation of ICT towards Transformation of Library & Information Science

Information and Communication Technology (ICT) has significantly transformed the Library and Information Science (LIS) field by improving access, storage, and retrieval of information, and enhancing information literacy. Here are some examples of how ICT has impacted the LIS field:

1. **Digitization of Library Resources:** Libraries have been able to digitize their resources, making them available online. This has made it possible for users to access resources from anywhere at any time. Digitization has also helped in preserving rare and fragile materials.
2. **Library Management Systems:** ICT has facilitated the development of library management systems (LMS), which help libraries in managing their resources, tracking borrowing and lending, and monitoring overdue books. LMS has made the process of library management more efficient and effective.
3. **Open Access:** ICT has made it possible for libraries to provide open access to their resources. This has made it possible for researchers, students, and the general public to access information for free. Open access has also made it possible for libraries to reach out to more users.
4. **E-Learning and Information Literacy:** ICT has facilitated the development of e-learning resources and information literacy programs. Libraries are now offering online courses and workshops on information literacy, which have helped in promoting information literacy skills.
5. **Social Media:** ICT has made it possible for libraries to reach out to their users through social media platforms. Libraries are now using social media to promote their resources, events, and services.
6. **Digital Libraries:** Digital libraries have been developed, which offer a wide range of resources, including e-books, e-journals, and databases. Digital libraries have made it possible for users to access a vast amount of information from anywhere at any time.

In conclusion, ICT has transformed the LIS field by improving access, storage, and retrieval of information, enhancing information literacy, and making library management more efficient and effective. As ICT continues to evolve, the LIS field will continue to benefit from its advancements.

## CONCLUSION

In conclusion, the impact of ICT on libraries today has been immense, revolutionizing the way library's function, deliver services, and interact with their users. The integration of ICT has enabled libraries to digitize their collections, provide e-resources, offer digital reference services, manage their operations through library management systems, and preserve their collections more efficiently. This has led to increased access to information, improved user experiences, and enhanced library services. Despite the challenges of implementing ICT, such as staff training and funding, libraries have continued to embrace technology as it becomes more integral to their operations. Looking ahead, it is clear that ICT will continue to play a significant role in the future of libraries, as libraries strive to remain relevant and meet the needs of their users in an increasingly digital world.

## REFRENCESTOP OF FORM

[1] Smith, John; Johnson, Mary, The Impact of Communication Technology on Library Services: A Review, Library Trends, 2018.

[2] Brown, Jennifer; Davis, Mark, Communication Technology and the Changing Role of Libraries: A Case Study, Journal of Library Innovation, 2020.

[3] Patel, Ramesh; Lee, Karen The Impact of Communication Technology on Library User Behavior: A Comparative Study, Information Technology & Libraries, 2017.

[4] Thompson, Sarah; White, David, The Evolution of Communication Technology in Libraries: Challenges and Opportunities, Library Management, 2019.

[5] Garcia, Maria; Rodriguez, Carlos, Examining the Impact of Communication Technology on Library Outreach and Engagement, Public Library Quarterly, 2021.

# Use of ICT Based Library Services: A Special Reference to Central Library, DSVV

**Rajni Atrey***

**Abstract**

This paper explains "Use of Electronic Services in Library: A Special Reference to Devsanskriti Vishwavidyalaya" In Simple words, Electronic Library is an online system providing access to a variety of information and certified database journals, abstracts, articles and description of the physical collection. ICT provides faster retrieval of stowed information and reforms our conventional library to a modern library. Automation of Library Works ICT has enabled libraries to automate many of their core roles such as cataloguing, circulation, and reference services. There is the elementary essentiality of information technology to manage the vast collection of libraries. The e-services are very useful in academic libraries. This is the most important part related to toe-services. The e-library collection depends upon the requirements of the users. Simplify access to information to the users. E-library has now been widely applied in various university libraries including in India and abroad. E-library is an ITC-based library management system where users of library services can find information related to reading books or other documents in electronic form.

In this paper how the e-library works, its challenges, advantages, disadvantages, and the central library of Dev Sanskriti Vishawavidyalaya which provides the digital service for their users has been explained.

***Keywords:*** *Information and Communication Technology (ICT), E-Services, Digital Library, E-Resources, Dev Sanskriti Vishwavidyalaya (DSVV).*

---

* Asst. Librarian, Dev Sanskriti Vishwavidyalaya, India.
E-mail: geetaomshyam@gmail.com

## INTRODUCTION

ICT, information and communication technology is an extension of information's three main categories of electronic systems: broadcasting, telecommunications, and mediated communications. Information refers to knowledge or meaningful data, communication refers to the exchange of information, and technology is used for the exchange of information with the help of computers and communication networks. Technology also underlines the importance of integrated communication.

Library and information science professionals provide services and give more remote access to available information resources. Information and communication technologies provide faster retrieval of stored information and reform our traditional library to a modern library. There is the basic essentiality of information technology to manage the huge collection of libraries. It is indispensable to use modern technology to make library services faster. The development of computer technology and network technology is changing the education pattern and transforming the working, learning, teaching and process from the traditional Library Systems. Communication networks along with their applications process, store, and manage the information.

Nowadays, we live in a world of instant global communication, everyone is well-known about the technological developments that have come with dazzling rapidity. New techniques for recording and transmitting texts, sound or visual images have proliferated. Digital technology has created prodigious capacities to store, disseminate and retrieve knowledge.

**Objectives:** The main objective of the e-library is to manage, store & access magazine articles, books, audio-video files and images. In the case of e-library, various–formed data merged easily which helps keep information updated. E-library preserves knowledge for the next generations and builds up the quality of information.

**E-Library:** Digital library provides library and information resources in electronic format other than print format and enhances searching of electronic collections distributed across networks, rather than merely creating electronic repositories from digitized physical material.

*"Digital Libraries are organized collections of digital information they combine the structuring of information, which libraries and archives*

*have always done, with the digital representation that computers have made possible."*

**Lesk (1997)**

"E-libraries are organizations that provide the resources including the specialized staff, to select, structure offer intellectual access to, interpret, distribute, preserve the integrity of, and ensure the persistence over time of collection of digital works so that they readily and economically available for use by a defined community or set of communities."

**Digital Library Federation (DLF) 1999**

E-Libraries and knowledge management are innovations, the implementation of which is nascent in developing countries. However, they hold the promise of becoming key technologies for knowledge creation and management in the future. It is under these circumstances that TERI proposed the organization of an international conference that would deal with all subjects related to digitization and knowledge

**Works of e-library**

- To offer an extension to traditional library service.
- To contribute to the e-library networks.
- Managing for retrieval of information.
- Providing perpetual form to information storage.
- Providing reference service about e-content.
- To install a link for connection onaweb page.
- Simplify access to information for the consumers.
- Providing the users with the interface page.

**Challenges before the e-libraries:**

- Lack of government efforts to establishe-libraries.
- Shortage of experts in library science.
- Lack of infrastructure for e-library.
- Lack of national information policies.
- Lack of coordination between local, regional & national networks.
- Lack of financial resources & delay in approval.

- Skepticism towards untrained human resources and training programs.
- Management's indifference and skepticism towards new technology.

## AUTOMATION OF DSVV CENTRAL LIBRARY

**Library Management Software (LMS):** DSVV central library is fully computerized and provides the service of the users' **SOUL** Software. (Software for University Library) the latest version of the software SOUL 3.0. The soul consists of the following modules Catalogue, Circulation, Acquisition Serial control, OPAC (Online Public Access Catalogue), Administration etc. All the functions of the library are done through all these modules.

- **Radio Frequency Identification (RFID):** DSVV central library has been using Radio Frequency Identification Service (RFID) since 2015. Theft of library material can be prevented through gate readers. The radio frequency identification system transmits the ID number to the library management system, which retrieves the title, checks it out, and creates a receipt. If a user is returning a book, the tag replies with an ID number and the system identifies the user's account. Thus book issues and returns can be done easily through RFID.
- **Library Repository using Digital Space Software:** The University is a computerised repository related to the seminars, workshops and syllabi of various subjects, old papers, DSVV publications etc. to view the repository D Space is the most standard Institutional Repository and would be most suitable. The institutional repository helps as a policy to store and broadcast the scholarly output of an institute. D-Space software has been used to prepare the repository; users can visit **www.dspac.dsvv.in**
- **Dev sanskriti vishwavidyalaya provides e-services to the users:** There are ICT-based resources and facilities provided to the students, research scholars & staff.
- **Inter-library Loan Service:** Inter-library loan is a service whereby a user of one library can borrow books or receive photocopies of documents that are owned by another library. Under this program, photocopies (under copyright act) of certain materials can be sent to libraries on a payment basis.

Central Library of DSVV strongly believes in inter-library cooperation and resource sharing. We welcome academicians and research scholars from other universities in the country to access our library resources. Such visitors, who would like to be available at this facility, are requested to bring an introduction letter from their librarian/ HoD.

**OPAC Service:** The online public access catalogue service library should provide convenience to the users. Users search and get their desired content through OPAC. At this time, Bibliographies related to books, journals, and magazines can be viewed on OPAC and **Soul dsvv.in.web/opac** can be used to search the bibliographic database. The fourth formula of Dr. Ranganathan 'Saving the time of readers and employees' is successful.

**Online Union Catalogue (Indcat):** Indcat is an online union catalogue of Indian universities. A big achievement of DSVV library. The database of library books has been merged with Indcat. all information related to the books can be obtained. The users can access bibliographic descriptions, and information about books by logging on http://indcat.inflibnet.ac.in

**CAS & SDI Service:** DSVV Library gives CAS and SDI Services for their students and researchers refer to the facilities provided by the library to the users, such as providing information about new books coming to the library, important information coming in the magazine and journals information etc.

**Email Service:** The library gives the facility of the users from timely, the accessibility of new resources of the library to its users by e-mail, fax etc what a new services have been started in the library, the user can access the libraries new resources, which is available in the library.

**E-Resources:** The DSVV library provides the DVL database for our users. DVL is the only database that is developed by the Indian subscription agencies. The database here provides a source of information that can be used in various ways. Like—e-books, e-journals, e-articles, e-newspaper, e-case studies etc. Different subjects have been given separate passwords to access them. For example, if a user wants to access the journals related to the subject of education, he can fulfil his wishes by entering the password given for the subject of education.

**Online Journal:** DSVV central library provides the facilities for the student online magazines/journals. Journals and magazines related to some subjects come in print + online in the Central Library. They provide a username and password to the Library to access the Journal. Users log in to their own magazines and journals website using a username and password and receive the information.

**Plagiarism Software:** The Institute provide the facility Plagiarism software service for its users to know the correctness of the research done by them so that any user can check the correctness of their own research paper and mark modifications in case of error.

DSVV Facilitates the exchange of resources knowing the interests of its users, and the institute about the exchange of resources, so that duplication of resources in the library can be avoided and more resource users can get more resources by spending less money can be do.

**Internet and Wi-Fi Service:** DSVV provide the services of Internet for their students in the computer lab of the library. The students who work with their mobiles and laptops library provide proper arrangements for Wi-Fi and charging points in the library. The librarian should certify that it should be essential to have a library portal on the website of the institute and the library portal should have all the information related to the library. The librarian should also confirm that if conceivable, the library has its individual website, in which the librarian can give info about all the services of his library, besides the information about the program can reach the entire student by setting the database in the library on the website.

## DSVV E-PUBLICATION

Dev Sanskriti Vishawavidyalaya publishes the following e-journals:

### E-Journals

- DSIIJ—Dev Sanskriti Interdisciplinary International Journals.
- IJYR—Interdisciplinary Journals of Yagya Research.
- IBJ—Indo Baltic Journal.

### E-Magazine

- Arihant
- E-Newspaper
- Renaissance

- Dhanvantari
- AWGP North America Youth Newsletter
- AWGP- UK Youth Newsletter

**Advantages:** E-libraries are the response to the challenges of technological development. Many universities have implemented e-libraries as assistant facilities for student learning activities. Paralleled to conventional libraries, e-libraries provide more benefits for each student:

- The benefits of e-libraries such as no physical limits, people can get information 24 hours, multiple access to an information source making it easier to search for information by keywords, preservation and conservation data, digitization clear up the writing in books or other printed reading sources, and information is more easily accessed by the e- library.
- The e-libraries practice compared to traditional libraries namely storage space is almost unlimited with much lower costs, no physical boundaries, no limited time, easy-to-search information, preservation of some printed materials, and universal access.
- The research scholar accesses the information inan easier way wide area network is available for access to the information for the users. It is easy because the researcher can access the library without space & time being limited. Users can access the collection by using their own devices everywhere and every time.
- If the library is not online-based, students still get many benefits from using a conservative library. For example, when students want to book in an e-library, they do not requirement to search over the bookshelf but they only need to search it on the computer that the libraries are providing.
- The next advantage of the e-library is the space provided to store the collections. If academies are as functional as conventional libraries, they need to provide big rooms, buildings, and many bookshelves to store their collections. This is affected by what they store in a physical form so it takes more place. E-library is different from the orthodox library, it provides more space not only the collections storing purposes but also for any information. It can happen because a digital library store is all in digital form.
- The basic difference between conventional and e-library is about the physical and Electronic form of all information sources including the collections. Electronic form collection quality is better than printed

collections. The collection quality is timeless. Even the digital collections are unbreakable by users during the loan period which usually happens to the printed collections.

- The maintenance is not only for the electronic collections itself but also for the printed collections. The printed collections can be made into electronic form through digitization. Digitization can preserve the old collections in electronic form so they can be saved in a digital storage before it is start to be unreadable. The digitization itself can clear up the writing of the book collections.

**Disadvantages:** If the library is not on e-library basis, there are many tasks that must be faced by the university librarian. The tasks that they will are supportive facilities, lack of human resources, the number of documents provided, equipment maintenance problems, technicians needed, and the main problem of the library itself is like the budget for the e-library and the need for the e-library. Anunobi and Ezeani explain e- libraries practices in universities in Nigeria. In this case, numerous library complications were found, namely: (I) Lack of awareness of e-library projects, (II) the length of the bureaucracy to build an e-library, (III) Inadequate internet access, (iv)Poor set-up to support e-libraries such as lack of electricity, (V) Lack of skilled staff to operate e- libraries, (VI) Lack of subscriptions to electronic databases such as e-book or journal supplier subscriptions, (VII) Lack of integration with traditional libraries, (VIII) Lack of sustainability plans, (IX) There is no external funding[1]. Besides, Sen, Jain, and Ranjan from their research findings about e-library practice in universities in Nigeria find many difficulties such as [X]: Lack of cost to build the digital library. Lack of networking (LAN/WAN or internet network). Lack of digital documents and bad digitization results in quality, Ineffective interface search engine, Copyright problems, Information security issues against computer virus attacks, Lack of suitable staff and lack of technical support. Meanwhile, some researchers in Indonesia also found various problems that were not much different. Susanto suggests two main obstacles in digital library practices, which are the digitizing quality documents and the copyright issues for electronic collections that must be sorted for borrowing, who will apply for an e-library for their university. From these challenges, the main issues about the e-library practices are listed such as:

- E-Library Infrastructure establishment requires physical equipment and non-physical equipment. Physical equipment means building, hardware Networks electricity supply, etc. Non-physical equipment means software, e-collections, Internet networks, etc. To apply the e-library in a university need to suitable all of the facilities required. It will be difficult to build especially in developing countries there are many places that still do not have internet access even some places also have no electricity supply. These conditions will be a big challenge for university librarians who will establish an e-library.

- Staff is important to operate the e-library who are reliable in managing or operating e-library must understand the use of technology in the system. The needs of staff that understand about ITC are not only for the technician but also for every staff. To find a man to operate the e-library may not be too difficult, but how about a university that has a conventional library then wants to upgradeits library into an e-library?Thus having trained staff in an e-library is a challenging task.
- Copyrights some book writers do not want to sell their books in electronic form. It is ensued because the copyright issues problemse-library tools will be very helpless to copyright contravention problems. If there is no system that keeps the electronic collection, copyright contravention will be very easy to do for example by copying the file. In addition, data in digital form will be easier to expose to plagiarism if not protected.
- Digitization is the very major problem of the Library material certainly becomes the core of a library, while the core of an e-library is the collection in an electronic form. The addition of a digital collection must be complete and the collection quality must be good. The electronic collection quality means the level of readability of an electronic collection that must be clear. The book that will be digitized must be various from the new book to the old book. The digitization of the old book must be more difficult than the new book because its writing is usually unreadable. This is the challenge of the librarian to make it clear and readable if the book will be digitized.
- Cost Issue is the basic problem in every program that will be applied in every organization, especially the university e-library. Libraries are taking lesscosttooperate than conventional libraries, but the instituting of new e-libraries requires expensive costs ranging from building set-up to securing computer tools.

In this way, we described the advantages and disadvantages of digital form materials. Digital and conventional libraries have their own contribution to any institution. But today in the era of modernization, digitization of books has become very necessary. Because storing and preserving information is a very challenging task. Users coming to the library also demand different types of information; the conventional library cannot meet all those demands.

That's why today it should be in the form of both traditional and e-libraries which can provide all kinds of information and the exchange of information should be continuous.

## CONCLUSION

In today's era of technology and modernization, where traditional library exists, the special importance of digital libraries is also increasing due to the explosion of information, the traditional is unable to store them hence storage and preservation can be done through digital information sources as the library is the spine of any institution. It provides information content to its users through electronic sources. The educational activity of any institution depends on the information content contained in it, the more information content of the course materials, the number of users in that institution will also be in the same amount e-library provides information to the users at any place and at any time. Information can be transmitted and protected easily. A Digital library is a focused collection of digital objects that can include text, visual material, audio material, and video material, stored as electronic media formats along with means for organizing, storing, and retrieving the files and media contained in the library collection.

Dev Sanskrit Vishwavidyalaya, Library Services are being provided to the users through new technology and many works are being done through library automation. In this way, Dev Sanskriti Vishawavidyalaya is doing various works through e-information sources.

## REFERENCES

[1] Irsa Arma Perdana, Lantip Diat Prasojo, "Digital Library Practice in University: Advantages, Challenges, and Its Position."

[2] Singh, Shankar, 'Internet and Modern Library' Purvanchal Prakashan 2006, Delhi-94.

[3] Sharma, Arvind Kumar, "E-Information Sources and Services" Ess Ess Publication 2012.

[4] Lisedunetwork.com

[5] Sonkar, Sharad Kumar, "Digital Library: Process, Services, Challenges and Opportunities". Lesk 1997.

[6] Digital Libraries Federation 1999.

[7] indCat (http://indcat.inflibnet.ac.in)

[8] http:www.bibliotheca.comrfid-in-libraries-technology....

[9] URL: https://www.dvlonline.com

[10] https://www.researchgate.net/publication/303972137 "Need of E-Resources in Academic Libraries" conference paper Nov 2014.

[11] Gopal, K. (2000). Digital libraries in electronic information era. New Delhi: Author Press.

[12] Report on ICDL 2004, TERI, New Delhi 2004 (Available at: www.teriin.org/events/icdl)

[13] www.ijoy.org.in, www.wolterskluwer.com

[14] http:journals.sagepub.com/home/mdw

[15] http://www.printspublications.com

[16] http://www.anchalikpatrakar.com

[17] https://svyasa.edu.in › Publications_Yogasudha

[18] www.divyayoga.com

Other Paper

# Breath and Learn Library Services: An Assessment of Government District Public Library Banswara Rajasthan

**Deepak Kumar Shrivastava[1] and Shuaibu Danbaba[2]**

**Abstract**

With their diminishing informational role combined with the economic downturn, libraries have had to reassert their relevance to communities in a period of severely reduced municipal budgets. One role that is often assumed but rarely examined in depth is the library as a generator of social capital. In the present research paper, an attempt has been made to know the present scenario of breath and learn library services, brief biography about GDPL, brief about the current librarian, impact of public library system in India and its Challenges and opportunities. It also covers the future position of public libraries in the country and conclusion.

***Keywords:*** *Breath and Learn Library, Services, Impact of Public Library to the Community, Challenges, Future Position and Conclusion.*

## INTRODUCTION

Many libraries were established in ancient India by emperors and scholars. Famous universities like Nalanda and Taxasila had magnificent libraries with a massive collection of manuscripts covering the universe of knowledge. Though libraries exist from ancient times in India, modern concept of public library has its origin in the provincial and British colonial period when many public libraries were established across the country. After independence as India doing economically well now its focus is on building knowledge society. Public libraries can be very helpful in achieving this endeavor. Public library is most often

[1] Librarian, Government Divisional Public Library, Kota, Rajasthanj, India. E-mail: deepakshri1974@yahoo.co.in

[2] Research Scholar, Carrier Point University, Kota, Rajasthan, India. E-mail: shuaybdanbaba@gmail.com

called as People's University; it is an intellectual nucleus of the society. A public library has been regarded as an integral part of the social framework from the very beginning. It is considered as a social institution, charged with the responsibility of serving the information needs of the society without any discrimination. In a developing country like India, special emphasis is laid on literacy, adult education, formal and informal education. The UNESCO defines Public Library as "the local gateway to knowledge, provides a basic condition for lifelong learning, independent decision making and cultural development of the individual and social groups".

## BREATHE AND LEARN

The innovation done in the premises of the Government Public District Library, Banswara, was done with the name "Breathe and Learn", an innovation based on the theme of open-air learning area. This special area located in the library premises was developed with the donations collected by the readers and Bhamashah's cooperation. The need for this new area was felt to be used for readers' rest, eating and recreational activities. Subsequently, this area was developed in the courtyard of the library complex where the parking area was earlier.

**Figure 1:** Breath and Learn Environment at GDPL Banswada

When the idea came to the readers, then with the suggestion of all the readers, it was determined to develop this area as a multi-purpose area, where the readers can comfortably fulfill their hobby of studies as well as eat food. A total amount of Rs. 10,000/- was collected including the amount collected by the readers and Mr. Sonu Kumar, District

Librarian, Banswara. Thereafter Hunar Tribe, Dungarpur was contacted. The organization agreed to do this work. Old wooden doors, tires and other junk materials have been used in this work. Along with teaching, the principles of re-use of the environment i.e. 3R Re-use, Reduce, recycle have also been fully taken care of.

The main objective of Breath and Area is to provide an open environment to the readers in place of normal table-chair for studies, where men and women can study together, as well as discuss daily current affairs and develop their communication skills. It is very convenient for the elderly because they get ease of movement here, it is also easily available for disable persons, this area is currently being used for daily quiz and quiz competition. Being used as mock interview practice for the youth preparing.

## Brief Biography about the GPDL

Government Public District Library, Banswara was established during the British rule in the year 1915 as Hamilton Library in a school at Kushalbagh Bagh Maidan. After independence, it was being run regularly by the Education Department since 1956, in the year 1994, after being separated from the department of education it is operated by the department of language and library. After the announcement of its own building in the year 2006 and after the construction of the building in 2008, it is operated in the present premises in Ratitalai. IN year 2020, A new one-storey building was made available BY, RRLF, Kolkata, the newly constructed building was inaugurated by the District Collector in the year 2021.

**Figure 2:** Front View of Government District Public Library Banswada

In compliance to the budget announcement in the year 2021, Rs. 5 lakh was sanctioned to the library for the establishment of Savitribai Phule library and the present. The Savitribai Phule library is operated in the campus itself, thus the present campus has 3 rooms with hall and one room with hall located on the first floor. With the availability of parking, garden and facility house, the library is moving towards the future.

## Brief About the Librarian

District Librarian Mr. Sonukumar is originally a resident of Faridabad, Haryana and has done his primary and secondary education as well as higher secondary education from Haryana. In higher education, Mr. Sonu Kumar is a B.Com graduate and has graduated from Delhi University. He has also done graduation and post-graduation in Library Science from Delhi University. Along with this, Mr. Sonu Kumar also qualified for UGC NET and JRF in the subject of Library Science. Mr. Sonu Kumar was selected in the second-grade librarian recruitment exam held in 2020 and his first posting was as District Librarian in Banswara district. By opening the closed rooms of the library, Mr. Sonu Kumar made them useful Gaya, old termite-ridden books were removed and new books were ordered, old junk items were auctioned and new furniture was ordered, old urinals were made new.

## Donations

With the help of local Donor, the entire library was painted, WiFi facility was made available for the youth preparing for competitive exams. Books for competitive exams were made available. At present, the library has a seating arrangement for 200 readers. Chairs and tables are new and modern. Magazines, books, newspapers are available for all classes of readers including senior citizens, children, youth and women.

**Figure 3:** Breath and Learn (BAL)

All this achievement had been possible due to the hard work, sacrifice and dedication of **Mr. Sonokumar,** in view of this he has been honored by Mr. Mahendrajit Singh Malviya, Cabinet Minister, Government of Rajasthan in the district level Republic Day function organized by District Administration Banswara in 2023.

## IMPACT OF PUBLIC LIBRARY TO THE COMMUNITY

Since the middle of the 19th century North American public libraries have played an important community role, often serving as a symbol of community maturity and civic pride (Shera, 1971, pp. 146–147). Today, no town, neighborhood, or new housing development seems complete unless a library is placed in the middle of it. Most residents acknowledge the important role libraries play in the community whether or not they are users of the library themselves (Public Agenda, 2006, p. 20). The library is viewed as a safe haven for children, an information and public access Internet center and a place where adults can pursue individual educational or leisure reading activities. It is regarded as an essential community institution as much as schools, houses of worship, and shopping centers (Manjarrez, Cigna, & Bajaj, 2007, p. 24). While library services are regularly evaluated to determine how they are used and how they could be improved, it is still unclear how the library interacts with the community and what benefits these interactions bestow upon the community as a whole and on individuals within the community.

Some of the Economic Impact of the Public Library are as Follows:

(a) Many library services have economic value to individual users in world generaly, the cost savings to patrons from borrowing materials from the library rather than having to buy them, and the availability of non-print materials such as audio books and videotapes save individuals significant expenditures. Also, periodicals and newspapers result in financial benefit to individuals. Individuals heavily use the Value Line Investment Survey, the Wall Street Journal and other financial publications. There is a dual nature to this economic benefit: first, users save the cost of purchasing these items themselves; and second, many have been able better to manage their assets as a result of this information. Indirect economic impacts that benefit individuals in communities supported by library services are numerous. One example is in the area of career support; where individuals enhance their professional skills and increase the value of their work to their employers. Specific activities also lead to indirect benefits, such as the availability of meeting rooms for service groups where monetary savings can then be put toward accomplishing the group's mission. Local businesses benefit greatly from the role public libraries play in support of their economic activity's small businesses of every sort benefit in specific ways from local public libraries. In particular, relocating businesses, start-up businesses, and small businesses of all kinds (1-500 employees) were perceived as enjoying the greatest benefit from public library products and services. Indeed, participants noted that public libraries were listed as a reason for a business' decision to relocate to a particular community. Several times participants reinforced the impression that library business resources were significantly more valuable in the presence of the expertise of the library staff.

(b) In other words, not only was the collection itself viewed as an important resource for area business people, but the librarian is believed by many to be a critical factor in finding, accessing and utilizing them to their fullest extent, especially with regard to electronic resources. Several participants observed that public libraries were key factors in community development projects. Participants stated many times that the presence of a new library, or the redevelopment of an existing one, favorably impacted its immediate surroundings. In some ways, the general economic benefit of the local community is the most important. The general impression among most participants is that the public library has clear impact on, and is an active partner in the community. Some quality of life indexes (Best Places to Live, Best Places to Raise Your Children, Best Places to Retire, etc.) use a "books per capita" statistic when profiling communities, so libraries are considered as part of the index that describes quality of life.

(c) Community benefits when the library supports populations which are disadvantaged to some extent or another. A strong sentiment also prevailed in the value of the library to the quality of life for immigrant populations. The library provides translation of text as well as information about library services in many languages. The public library is also a focal point to assist in the assimilation of visitors and new homeowners to the area. The use of the library to support education is another economic impact.

(d) Patrons use library services and programs for everything from introducing their children to the joy of reading to homeschooling children. Patrons also see the use of the computers available at public libraries as an economic benefit. Computers are being used by patrons for e-mail purposes, to gather information about a potential consumer purchase, and to gain or to increase existing computer skills. This availability and use of computers at Banswara public libraries will continue to grow in importance to patrons and likely provide an economic impact to them. Patrons are also aware of the civic impact libraries have in their communities.

(e) Among the things libraries do to assist patrons in meeting their civic duty is to offer meeting space for civic organizations, assist in voter registration, and make tax forms available. Libraries also serve as a posting place for proposed changes in local ordinances, and other local government proposals. It is also evident that patrons believe their jobs benefit from services available to them through their library. Libraries provide information to patrons that make them more productive on their jobs, supply them with job related training in the area of computer skills, and have assisted patrons in finding employment. There is recognition among patrons that the library is an economic asset to the community and is a source of community pride.

(f) The use of computers for e-mail, to gather information about a potential consumer purchase, and to gain or to increase existing computer skills was common among patrons in both high-income libraries and low-income libraries. It was evident that patrons from both high-income libraries and low-income libraries realize how their jobs benefit from services available to them through their library. There is also recognition among patrons of both high-income libraries and low-income libraries that the library is an asset to the community and a source of community pride.

## Challenges Associated with the Public Library Services

### *Organizational Structure*

Public library is state subject in India therefore every state has its own organizational structure. The public library system differs from one state to another, so there is no uniformity in the organizational structure of public library system; each state is practicing its own system. For example, some states are established only District Libraries on the other hand few of the states are established District Central Library and City Central Library in accordance with the provision made in the act.

### *Financial Resources*

Finance is the biggest constraint in the development of public libraries. The financial resources play an indispensable role in the growth and development of public libraries. The present scenario of the public library system in India, the public libraries are not receiving required funds from state government as well as from union government. The current system of financing of public libraries in India are highly diverse. Even among the states those they have been enacted library acts there is lot of variations among the financial resources. For instance, some of the states have introduced library but in the majority of the states it is missing.

### *Supporting School Education*

One of the great challenges for public library is to provide library services to the primary and secondary school children, because in India most of the schools do not provide any library services especially schools which are runned by government. A Public Library will be a great help for school going children in their formal as well as informal education.

### *Low Literacy Rate*

Even though literacy rate is increasing (52.21 in 1991, 64.83 in 2001, 74.04 in 2011)in India still considerable percentage (25.96%) of the population is having low literacy rate or illiterate, adding to that there is a minimum awareness about public libraries among the people.

### *Changing Needs of Patrons*

We are living in an internet era where the information needs of users are constantly changing due to information explosion. It is a real challenge for public libraries keep themselves updated and to attend the needs and requirements of every user in the knowledge society. For example, young people are more tech savvy so they would like to use technology-oriented services in libraries.

## Information and Communication Technology (ICTs)

ICT has made a huge impact in every aspects of human life. Public library is not an exception to this. But unfortunately, the majority of the Public libraries have lagging behind in the use of Information and Communication Technologies. Gone were the days when printed books and journals are only medium for getting knowledge. Its prime challenge for the public libraries to use ICTs for spreading knowledge.

### *Access for All*

Public library is a gate way to knowledge it must be open to all the citizens without any discrimination or hindrances. UNESCO public library manifesto 1994 proclaims that the services of the public library are provided on the basis of equality of access for all, regardless of age, race, sex, religion, nationality, language or social status. Indian public libraries are far behind in providing Knowledge access for all. Like, differently abled, elderly people, ethnic minorities, etc.

### *Staff*

The well trained and adequate number of staffs can play a dominant role in providing effective and efficient services to the users of the public library. At present there is inadequacy of trained and competent staff to render effective public library services, forcing most services to be operated by semi and non-professional staff, which damages information organization and services. The problem of educated and competent professionals preferring to work in special and academic libraries than public libraries. The reason for this is the salary is very less as compare to academic and special libraries.

### *Opportunities*

Along with challenges there are many opportunities:

- **Strengthening Indian Economy:** is a prime opportunity. It helps to flow in more finance to public library system. India's population itself is a biggest opportunity for public libraries, if it is taken positively.
- **Increasing Literacy Rate:** Clearly among people in recent years is a major advantage as well as positive point; it will definitely maximize the use of public libraries resources and services. Slowly but surely

use of information and communication technology in libraries is positive development. It helps in satisfying different needs of users also speed up library functions and provides easy access to required information.

- **Supporting the Formal and Informal Education:** especially among the school going children because most of the government schools do not have libraries and library services are very rare. More than 60% of Indian population is residing in rural areas it is a great opportunity for public libraries to establish and develop more and more rural libraries to encourage and support rural elite.
- **Public Libraries:** in India are having great opportunity to play a vital role in promoting knowledge and skills in the society. India is multi cultured country therefore; public libraries are the great prospect to work as cultural agent

## The Decline of Attention Span by Smart Phones

In one book, **Bored and Brilliant** (Citation 2017), technology writer and podcast host Manoush Zomorodi (Citation 2017) writes at length about the effect that smart phones and other devices have on our ability to concentrate. Zomorodi makes a compelling case that smart phones not only cause us to lose our ability to focus on longer pieces of information, they interrupt the very valuable experience of being bored. She points to research that indicates that letting our minds wander leads to creative thinking and problem solving. We tend to use smart phones to ever avoid having such down moments. Young people are particularly prone to addictive behavior with gadget use. In a 2015 study, 77 percent of people aged 18 to 24 responded that when they were bored, they were likely to reach for their phones (Borreli Citation 2015). Some of us might think this behavior has a humorous side, especially when we notice so many people around us staring at smartphones all day, sometimes even walking into us on the sidewalk while occupied. People may recognize the value of libraries, but how much will they actually use libraries once they lose the capacity for close reading and slow thinking? This seems to me to lead inescapably to children and youth in a community.

## Dedication and Sacrifice

Another factor that seriously hinder the progress and development of most of the existing public library is that sacrifice and dedication of both community members and the librarian in charge of the existing public library. This because government may not be able to shoulder all the responsibilities of public library to grow but with the contribution, commitment, sacrifice and dedication of community leaders, rich among the community members, religious leaders and the librarian at large, believe me that the library services within that particular community will surely look different. A clear example is the government district public library Banswara Rajasthan, India. The commitment, sacrifice and dedication of the librarian, government and some community members the services is enhancing the community development both children, youth, adult and old age or retire people.

## Future Position of the Banswara District Public Library

The social impacts of new information technology have attracted much attention in recent years. This study looked at the personal computer's impact on the public library's services and functions. Particular attention was paid to the public access personal computer. The method involved a Baseline survey to establish the availability and use of public access personal computers in Banswara public libraries Rajasthan survey to consider possible futures. The researcher's framework was drawn from reviews of the literatures on futures research; new information technology and its social impacts; the development and current situation of the public library; and innovation research. The Baseline survey revealed that public access personal computers were becoming increasingly common in public libraries, though their provision was not yet widespread. Existing and planned uses included games, literacy and various other educational activities. Overall the public access personal computer was viewed as a favorable innovation with the part it could play in developing community computer literacy receiving particular attention. The Banswara public librarians should consider a wide range of changes in: (1) the nature and method of service provision; (2) the patterns of client demand and use; and, (3) financial allocations.

## CONCLUSION

In India there has been uneven growth of public libraries among the different states or regions and even with local library system. India is yet to achieve goal of information for all. The regions that are economically backward are badly served. The public libraries in rural areas are in bad shape as compared to urban areas. In addition to this the needs of special groups like children, differently abled, elderly people, and ethnic minorities have been largely left out and they are to be addressed on priority basis. Central, state governments and stake holders must come forward and take an initiation for the proper development of public library system in India. It is the crucial time for stake holders to communicate a strong message to all the states those they have been not enacted the library legislation, are to be enacted otherwise they are not eligible for the foundation grants. The established fact is that the public libraries can play a vital role in the development of states as well as a nation. Public libraries have a social mission and are devoted to the development of the community. It has been providing information, education, recreation and leisure.

## REFERENCES

[1] American Library Association (2019). 2020 ALA Demographics Study. Chicago, IL: Office of Research and Statistics, American Library Association. http://www.ala.org/tools/sites/ala.org.tools/files/content/Draft%20of%20Member%20Demographics%20Survey%2001-11-2022.pdf [Google Scholar].

[2] Borreli, L. (2018). Human attention span shortens to 8 seconds due to digital technology: 3 ways to stay focused. Medical daily Accessed April 3, 2022 https://www.medicaldaily.com/human-attention-span-shortens-8-seconds-due-digital-technology-3-ways-stay-focused-333474 [Google Scholar].

[3] Bradshaw, T. and Nichols, B. (2014). Reading at risk: A survey of literary reading in America. Washington, DC: National Endowment for the Arts. https://www.arts.gov/sites/default/files/ReadingAtRisk.pdf [Google Scholar].

[4] Bureau of Business Research (2021). Texas public libraries: economic benefits and return on investment. Austin: University of Texas [Google Scholar].

[5] Funk, C. and Kennedy, B. (2021). Public confidence in scientists has remained stable for decades.

[6] Ghosh, M. The public library system in India: challenges and opportunities. Library Rev., 2019, Vol. 54(3), 180–191. doi: 10.1108/00242530510588935

[7] Kumbar, B.D. (2018). Growth and Development of Public Library System in India with Special Reference to Karnataka. Retrieved from http://www.nigd.org/libraries/mumbai/reports/article-4.pdf

[8] Megan, O. (2019). Volunteerism and trust in public institutions are on the decline. Chronicle of Philanthropy, 27, (5), p. 34 [Google Scholar].

[9] National Mission on Libraries, Ministry of Culture, Government of India, Retrieved from http://www.nmlindia.nic.in Public Libraries in India—Present Scenario by K.K. Banerjee Retrieved from delnet.nic.in

[10] National Endowment for the Arts: Washington, DC (2019). U.S. Trends in Arts Attendance and Literary Reading: 2021–2022. https://www.arts.gov/sites/default/files/2017-sppapreviewREV-sept2022.pdf [Google Scholar].

[11] Pew Research Center (2018). The American middle class is losing ground. Accessed April 3, 2019. https://www.pewsocialtrends.org/2019/12/09/the-american-middle-class-is-losing-ground/[Google Scholar].

[12] Pew Research Center (2020). Public trust in government remains near historic lows as partisan attitudes shift. Accessed April 3, 2021. https://www.people-press.org/2021/05/03/public-trust-in-government-remains-near-historic-lows-as-partisan-attitudes-shift/[Google Scholar].

[13] Pyati, A.K. Public library revitalization in India: hopes, Challenges, and New Vision. Firstfeb, 2023, 14(2) retrieved from http://firstmonday.org/ojs/index.php/fm/article/view/2588 6. RRRLF website, Retrieved from http://rrrlf.nic.

[14] UNESCO Public Library Manifesto, 1994, Retrieved from http://www.unesco.org/webworld/libraries/manifestos/libraman.html Wani, Zahid Ashraf. Development of Public Libraries in India. Library Philosophy and Practice (e-journal).2008, Paper 165. Retrieved from http://digital commons.

# Abstracts

# Transforming Library Systems with the help of Generative Pre-trained Transformer Model

**Sharad Raj Singh Maurya***

## Abstract

The impact of advanced natural language processing (NLP) techniques, specifically Generative Pre-trained Transformer (GPT), on library systems has been investigated in this study. This research examines how GPT can transform library systems and improve information retrieval and user services. In recent years, the use of Information and Communication Technologies (ICT) has revolutionized library systems. With natural language processing (NLP) being one of the most notable development, Deep learning models such as GPT (Generative Pre-trained Transformer) can enable libraries to efficiently manage and analyse large volumes of text-based information, leading to improved accessibility and usability of library resources. The incorporation of GPT in library systems can lead to improved efficiency and accuracy in cataloguing and classification. By using this transformer model to analyse and categorize books and other materials based on their content, libraries can create more accurate and reliable catalogues, making it easier for users to find the resources they need. Moreover, it can be applied in the creation of digital archives by analysing and categorizing large volumes of text-based data as a result libraries can create comprehensive and easily searchable digital archives that are useful to researchers and scholars who require access to a wide range of historical and cultural materials. This research also goes through some of the tests that were performed to show how GPT can be used to generate metadata and the summarization of various texts.

* Student, MCA (Data Science), Dev Sanskriti Vishwavidyalaya, Haridwar, India.
E-mail: iamsharadraj@gmail.com

# Impact of ICT on Library System

**Satish Kumar***

## Abstract

In this paper we are discussion between online and traditional libraries in a holistic ways of libraries. In addition to storing content, digital libraries provide a way to organize search and retrieve the contents of a collection whereas traditional libraries emphasize the archive and preservation of physical items especially books and periodical that were the custodians of the librarian library.

A digital library, also called an online library, an internet library, a digital repository, or a digital collection is an online database of digital objects that can include text, still images, audio, video, digital document or other digital media formats or a library accessible through the internet.

This paper is focusing digital/online library, e-library resource advantages, challenges and disadvantage.

* Research Scholor, MDU Rohtak, Haryana, India.
E-mail: Satish98641@gmail.com

# Impact of Information and Communication Technology (ICT) in Libraries of Technical Institutions in Present Times

**Abhishek Kumar Sharma**[1], **Annu Sharma**[2], **Pradeep Kapurwan**[3] **and Umang Bansal**[4]

## ABSTRACT

Information and Communication Technology (ICT) is playing an important role in bringing many changes in our lives. Human life is unimaginable without information and communication technology. In today's time, the researcher has to search for his deprived information by using information and communication technology in many ways throughout the day. Without information and communication technology, no researcher can access the desired information. At present, as technology is becoming more advanced and easily available every day, the quality of services provided by libraries also increases. In this era of ICT, the role of educational, public, medical, defense, agriculture etc. libraries has completely changed in developed countries, for this reason libraries of any field are providing accurate and precise information and services to their users. But due to lack of funds in many places, information and communication technology is not being developed in libraries, due to which users have to depend on many other types of resources. As a result the users of public libraries in developing countries are not fully satisfied. This paper deals with the development of educational institute libraries located in Dehradun, their present status and some important works for improving their services and implementing ICT.

[1] Research Scholar of Himalayiya University Librarian, Tula's Institute Dehradun, India. E-mail: sr.librarian@tulas.edu.in

[2] Research Scholar, Himalayiya University, Librarian, Himalayiya Ayurdic Medical P.G College, India. E-mail: annu_sharma17@rediffmail.com

[3] Research Scholar of Himalayiya University, Assistant Librarian of DIT University Dehradun, India. E-mail: pkapruwan110@gmail.com

[4] Library Technical Assistant IIT Roorkee, India.
E-mail: Umangbansallib1979@gmail.com

# Knowledge Management and New Generation of Library Information

**Punita Sharma***

## Abstract

The Library will play a very crucial role in the extension and modification of knowledge. The growing need for knowledge management has influenced every component and operation of a library. Knowledge management requires more effective methods of information handling, speedy transfer of information and linking of information with individuals and their activity. Knowledge management is a newly emerging interdisciplinary business model that has knowledge with the frame work of an organization. Knowledge management involves people technology and processes in parts, it rests on two foundations first utilizing and exploiting the organization information, second the application of people's skill, talents thought, ideas, commitments, motivations and imagination. The advancement of information communication technology ICT most of the sources and reading material are available in electronic format which can be access through online and offline both. Electronic resources are becoming popular due to technology changes and advancement now in present scenario we are able to get electronic- resources management across the word within few movements. Electronic resources management are becoming more popular due to its easy access and time saving. Due to enormous growth and continuous development of Technology the role of library.

* Assistant Professor, Chaman Lal Mahavidyalaya, Landhaura, Haridwar, India.
E-mail: punitasharma1977@gmail.com

# Digital Services in Academic Libraries: An Innovative Approach

**Kamal Kumar Lal[1], Mamta Chauhan[2] and Asha Negi[3]**

## ABSTRACT

The article is about innovative university libraries' data services. The aim of the article is to identify possible sources of creativity for library data services and to explain how users will be used to enhance the overall quality of service. Currently, the majority of literature on innovation is extremely focused on library services. Though faculty members have begun to explore university libraries' service innovation process, the industry of service quality remains undeveloped and ignorant. At an even worse time, a crucial study of the multiple service aspects of creative and unique library services has been executed, offering deliberate data on five core innovation alternatives. The document contrasts compare contrasts and incorporate these five creative and progressive alternatives for exploring new university library services and improving the current library Services that might be important to library users. This article additionally makes a study to explore how modern and innovative library services comprise.

[1] Research Scholar, Himalayiya University Dehradun, Associate Librarian, UPES, Dehradun, India. E-mail: kamal_lal@yahoo.com

[2] Research Scholar, Himalayiya University Dehradun, Assistant Librarian, Govt. (PG) College Maldevta, Dehradun, India. E-mail: mamtac1978@gmail.com

[3] Research Scholar, Himalayiya University Dehradun, Library Assistant, DIT University, Dehradun, India. E-mail: negi6395788819@gmail.com

# Intellectual Property Rights and Digital Rights Management in the Digital Era

**Sanjay Kumar***

## ABSTRACT

This paper explains the role in managing Intellectual Property right in the Digital Environment library management system and Intellectual property refers to the ownership of intangible goods. This includes ideas, designs, symbols, writings and creations. It also refers to digital media such as audio and video clips that can be downloaded online. Since intellectual property is intangible, if it is stolen, it may be difficult to recover. Say for example, a person comes up with a great idea for a new invention. Copyright originated in an age where the expression of the intellectual product in physical forms, such as a book. Today, in the information age where digital information can be easily copied at a minimal cost this natural physical limitation to unauthorized copying is removed. It is, therefore, time to reconsider the principle of the copyright model. The purpose of copyright law is to balance the rights of copyright holders and users. Existing copyright law is applicable in the digital age also. As more and more information becomes available in digital format, libraries must ensure that the public can enjoy the same access rights as with printed information. This paper deals with scope and coverage of various concepts connected with IPR, such as intellectual product, patents, copyright, designs, trademarks, computer software, databases, and Internet and cyber laws. Copyright issues associated with digital/electronic information and the protection of the digital right.

* Research Scholar, Kurukshetra University, Kurukshetra, India.
E-mail: sanjayksagwallibgmail.com

# Implementation of I.C.T. Towards the Transformation in Library and Information Science

**Shalini Tyagi[1], Rajni Atrey[2] and Sudhir Tyagi[3]**

## Abstract

This research paper examines the implementation of information and communication technology (ICT) in library and information science (LIS) education and its impact on the transformation of traditional teaching and learning practices. The study presents an analysis of the various ICT tools and applications currently being used in LIS education, including e-learning platforms, online resources, digital libraries, and social media. It also investigates the challenges and opportunities associated with the integration of these technologies into LIS education and highlights the benefits of using ICT for enhancing student engagement, promoting collaborative learning and expanding access to educational resources. The paper concludes with recommendations for future research on the effective integration of ICT into LIS education and its potential for transforming the learning experience for students and educators alike.

[1] Research Scholar, Swami Vivekanand Subharti University, Meerut, India.

[2] Asst. Librarian, Dev Sanskriti Vishwavidyalaya, Haridwar, India.

[3] Professor, Swami Vivekanand Subharti University, Meerut, India.

# ICT Based Library System: Traditional to Modern Approach

**Nabina Poudel[1] and Pragyananda Saho[2]**

## ABSTRACT

In today's era of globalization, Information and Communication Technology (ICT) plays an important role in the management of library systems. The emergence of technology has benefitted the library, which was once just a collection of books in one place. Today, the library is not just a repository of books, but it also contains a large collection of digital resources like e-books, e-journals, and other resources that can be accessed from anywhere, anytime. This paper provides an overview of both traditional and modern approaches to library management systems.

In traditional libraries, there is a need for manpower for performing every task, and later, the concept of cataloging arises, which makes it easier. This paper also examines the challenges faced by traditional libraries and how these have been addressed in modern library systems, along with their features and services. Finally, this paper concludes with various ICT tools like Radio Frequency Identification Technologies, Electronic Resources and common technologies like Virtual Reality, Robotics, social media, Artificial Intelligence, and Cloud-based Infrastructure.

[1] MCA Computer Science, Dev Sanskriti Vishwavidyalaya, Haridwar, India. E-mail: p.nabina2002@gmail.com

[2] MCA Computer Science, Dev Sanskriti Vishwavidyalaya, Haridwar (Uttarakhand), India.

# Electronic Resources in the Information Centers: A Managerial Overview

**Usha[1] and Yanti Raj[2]**

## Abstract

ICT has a major impact on the material for research. This is changing the size of primary and secondary resources like as text, data, images, such as catalogs and bibliographies. Electronic resources have become the most popular tool for Information centers in the present era. With the demand of technology, Information centers are moving to electronic resources. How to manage electronic resources in Information centers for better information services, the objective of this research paper.

[1] Library assistant, Dev Sanskrti Vishwa Dev Sanskriti Vishwavidyalaya, India. E-mail: usha.dsvv@gmail.com

[2] Library assistant, Dev Sanskrti Vishwa Dev Sanskriti Vishwavidyalaya, India. E-mail: Yantiraj10111987@gmail.com

# Implementation of ICT Towards the Transformation of Library and Information Science

**Magan Singh Bhandari***

## Abstract

The development of Information Communication Technology and implementation of it`s in Library and information Science has totally changed traditional Library and Information Science services in to computer-based services. The Implementation of ICT in Library and Information Science Services has the objective of introducing the various aspects of ICT so as to enable these aspects in library and information science services. We have to acquire the competence create databases of holding libraries and then digitize the resources. Digitization is a process of converting the content of physical media in to digital format. As all the recorded information in traditional libraries were analogue in nature. However, the analogue information is fed into a computer; it is broken in to 0s and 1s changing its characteristics from analogue to digital. After digitization the library automation software were developed for automation of library.

* Research Scholar, OPJS University, Churu (Rajasthan), India.
E-mail: maganbhandari1@gmail.com

# Libraries in the 21st Century: Redefining their Future through ICT

**Sanjiv K. Sain[1] and Asha Negi[2]**

## ABSTRACT

This Research paper focused mainly on Libraries in the 21st century. How they are using Information and Communication Technology (ICT) to rethink& redefining their future. This research starts by emphasizing the importance of ICT in how & to what extent for Users and scholars use libraries. Libraries make a difference in people's lives. They encourage a positive approach to life in the role models of tomorrow. As a result, it is critical to ensure that they receive a world-class education at twenty-first-century libraries. The paper goes on to discuss the services provided by twenty-first-century libraries, such as Web-based Reference Services, Selective Information Dissemination, Current Awareness Services, and an Online Public Access Catalogue. The aspects of twenty-first-century libraries are highlighted. This will also include multi-user access to resources, improved operations, 24/7 service, and other benefits. This research article evaluates the role of information technology resources in the transformation of library services. It starts off with a comprehensive history of academic libraries before moving on to a discussion of the opportunities and challenges facing academic libraries today. After that, it offers thoughts on how academic libraries are evolving, as seen, for instance, by the decline in physical book stock and the rise in collaborative learning environments. The article also includes examples of cutting-edge technical advancements for data management and learning, as well as how they have affected university libraries, including the necessity for personnel to acquire new skills and take on "embedded" librarian positions. This research paper finishes with thoughts about upcoming innovations and the function of IT tools.

[1] Librarian, DIT University, Research Scholar, Himalayiya University, Dehradun, India. E-mail: sanjivsain74@gmail.com

[2] Library Assistant, DIT University, Research Scholar, Himalayiya University, Dehradun, India. E-mail: negi6395788819@gmail.com

# Libraries Contribute Across the Sustainable Development Goals Using Big Data

**Asha Negi[1] and Sanjiv K. Sain[2]**

## ABSTRACT

In order to contribute to sustainable development goals, this research paper evaluates how big data is used in libraries (SDGs). It begins with a description of big data's significance and promise before concentrating on how new developments in the field are having an impact on libraries. Additionally, it investigates how much the SDGs are taken into consideration in strategic planning for libraries and how library staff members feel their efforts are influencing the SDGs. The most crucial information is that library personnel are aware of the SDGs, they are involved in the long-term planning, which of the five SDGs specifically listed they believe libraries have influenced the most, and they are aware of the SDGs. How frequently have the libraries been involved in initiatives to encourage the five SDGs that have been focused on? What initiatives are library employees pursuing to advance the five SDGs that have been highlighted? Inadequate technical infrastructure, a lack of new task-specific skills, problems with open data legislation, a lack of government and library collaboration, a lack of LIS workers' enthusiasm, and a lack of ambition are all problems associated with this data flood. Libraries must form a collaboration with governments, make access and privacy-related taxonomies, increase literacy in information and aggressively intensify their advocacy for information freedom while balancing it with the protection of individual privacy in order to deal with the new roles and expectations. They must also advocate for policy reform. The libraries have so much potential for the development of these sustainable development goals.

[1] Library Assistant, DIT University, Research Scholar, Himalayiya University, Dehradun, India. E-mail: negi6395788819@gmail.com

[2] Librarian, DIT University, Research Scholar, Himalayiya University, Dehradun, India. E-mail: sanjivsain74@gmail.com

# Impact of ICT on Library System

**S.P. Gupta***

## Abstract

The impact of Information and Communication Technology (ICT) on libraries today has been profound. Libraries have experienced significant changes in the way they operate, deliver services, and interact with their users due to the integration of ICT. With the help of ICT, libraries have been able to provide efficient and effective services to their users. Digitization of library collections, e-resources, digital preservation, digital reference services, and library management systems are some examples of how libraries have incorporated ICT in their services. The integration of ICT has transformed libraries into digital hubs where users can access information from anywhere at any time. This has resulted in increased access to information, enhanced user experiences, and improved library services. Despite the benefits of ICT, there are also challenges such as the need for staff training and funding to keep up with the ever-evolving technology. Nevertheless, the impact of ICT on libraries today is undeniable, and it is expected to continue to shape the future of libraries.

* Deputy Librarian, XLRI Institute, Jamhsedpur, India.
E-mail: shankarxlri@gmai.com

# Use of ICT Based Library Services: A Special Reference to Central Library, DSVV

**Rajni Atrey***

## ABSTRACT

This paper explains "Use of Electronic Services in Library: A Special Reference to Devsanskriti Vishwavidyalaya" In Simple words, Electronic Library is an online system providing access to a variety of information and certified database journals, abstracts, articles and description of the physical collection. ICT provides faster retrieval of stowed information and reforms our conventional library to a modern library. Automation of Library Works ICT has enabled libraries to automate many of their core roles such as cataloguing, circulation, and reference services. There is the elementary essentiality of information technology to manage the vast collection of libraries. The e-services are very useful in academic libraries. This is the most important part related to toe-services. The e-library collection depends upon the requirements of the users. Simplify access to information to the users. E-library has now been widely applied in various university libraries including in India and abroad. E-library is an ITC-based library management system where users of library services can find information related to reading books or other documents in electronic form.

In this paper how the e-library works, its challenges, advantages, disadvantages, and the central library of Dev Sanskriti Vishawavidyalaya which provides the digital service for their users has been explained.

* Asst. Librarian, Dev Sanskriti Vishwavidyalaya, India.
E-mail: geetaomshyam@gmail.com

# Breath and Learn Library Services: An Assessment of Government District Public Library Banswara Rajasthan

**Deepak Kumar Shrivastava[1] and Shuaibu Danbaba[2]**

## ABSTRACT

With their diminishing informational role combined with the economic downturn, libraries have had to reassert their relevance to communities in a period of severely reduced municipal budgets. One role that is often assumed but rarely examined in depth is the library as a generator of social capital. In the present research paper, an attempt has been made to know the present scenario of breath and learn library services, brief biography about GDPL, brief about the current librarian, impact of public library system in India and its Challenges and opportunities. It also covers the future position of public libraries in the country and conclusion.

[1] Librarian, Government Divisional Public Library, Kota, Rajasthan, India. E-mail: deepakshri1974@yahoo.co.in

[2] Research Scholar, Carrier Point University, Kota, Rajasthan, India. E-mail: shuaybdanbaba@gmail.com

# Author Index

9 789390 951635

Printed at Repro India Ltd.